Cognitive and Dialectical Behavioral Therapy

Overcome Anxiety and Depression, Tackle Negative Thought Patterns, Control Your Emotions, and Change Your Mood Through Effective Psychotherapy

By

Elizabeth Broks

© Copyright 2019 – Elizabeth Broks - All rights reserved.

The content contained within this book may not be reproduced, duplicated or transmitted without direct written permission from the author or the publisher.

Under no circumstances will any blame or legal responsibility be held against the publisher, or author, for any damages, reparation, or monetary loss due to the information contained within this book. Either directly or indirectly.

Legal Notice:

This book is copyright protected. This book is only for personal use. You cannot amend, distribute, sell, use, quote or paraphrase any part, or the content within this book, without the consent of the author or publisher.

Disclaimer Notice:

Please note the information contained within this document is for educational and entertainment purposes only. All effort has been executed to present accurate, up to date, and reliable, complete information. No warranties of any kind are declared or implied. Readers acknowledge that the author is not engaging in the rendering of legal, financial, medical or professional advice. The content within this book has been derived from various sources. Please consult a licensed professional before attempting any techniques outlined in this book.

By reading this document, the reader agrees that under no circumstances is the author responsible for any losses, direct or indirect, which are incurred as a result of the use of information contained within this document, including, but not limited to, — errors, omissions, or inaccuracies.

Table of Content

Introduction..9

Chapter 1: Understanding CBT 13

  Basics of CBT 13
     1. Core Beliefs 14
     2. Dysfunctional Assumptions 14
     3. Negative Automatic Thoughts (NAT) 15

  Aims of CBT 15

  Techniques and Methods Used 16

Chapter 2: Understanding and Identifying Issues That Arise in Everyday Life 19

  What is Anxiety? 20

  Depression.. 23

  Principles of Automatic Intrusive Thoughts 24
    Properties of Automatic Intrusive Thoughts 25

  Origin of Unwanted Thoughts 26

  The Thought-Feeling-Action Connection 27

Chapter 3: Getting Your Life Back: Proven CBT Techniques 29

  Set a Goal... 29

  Evaluate Your Goals.. 32

  Deal with Your Pessimistic Thoughts 33

  Conclusion... 35

Chapter 4: Reshaping Your Attitude.................. 36

  Want to Be More Positive? Practice Gratitude 37

Stop for a Minute and Write Down Ten Things You are Thankful for and Then Come Back to Me 38

Become a Positive Hero 39

Case Study 40

Conclusion.. 41

Chapter 5: Recognizing and Modifying Your Belief Systems 43

Step 1: Identify If Your Mentality Is Stable Or Changes With Your Moods 44

Step 2: Emphasize the Positive Thoughts That You Have About Yourself to Divert From Negative Ideas 44

Step 3: Start a Positive Thought Journal.......... 45

Step 4: Re-Evaluate Yourself 45

Step 5: Tell an Accountability Partner 46

Step 6: Try to Discover Where the Old Thoughts Came From 46

Step 7: Watch Yourself Whenever You Spiral Into Negative Self-Talk 47

Step 8: Evaluate How Much You Accept Negative Thoughts or Beliefs 47

Conclusion.. 48

Chapter 6: Dealing with Worry and Anxiety 49

Fight-or-Flight Response 49

Structured Problem-Solving 50

Try to Limit Your Consumption of Technology and Messaging Tools 50

Try Meditation Techniques and Aromatherapy 50

Take a Hot Bath/Shower to Try Aquatherapy .. 51

Exercise 51

Dealing with Procrastination 52

Conclusion 53

Chapter 7: Getting Rid of Negativity in Your Life *54*

What is Negativity? 54

Where Do Negative Thoughts Come From? 54

Effects of Having Negative Thoughts 55

Case Study 64

Conclusion 66

Chapter 8: The Emergence of Dialectical Behavioral Therapy (DBT) *68*

Origins of Dialectical Behavioral Therapy 69

Principles of DBT 71

Four DBT Strategies 72
   Mindfulness 72
   Distress Tolerance 73
   Interpersonal Strategies 73
   Regulation of Negative Emotions 73

Conclusion 73

Chapter 9: Understanding Borderline Personality Disorder (BPD) *75*

What is Borderline Personality Disorder?....... 75
Symptoms of BPD 76
Negative Self-Image..76
Emotional Insecurity..76
Risky Behavior...77
Eating Disorders..77

Causes of BPD 78
Negative and Traumatic Experiences...................78
Brain Chemistry..78
Family History 78

Getting Treatment for BPD 79
Dealing with Triggers and BPD 79
Common Triggers 80
Cognitive Triggers...80
Managing Triggers.. 81
Case Study 81

Conclusion.. 82

Chapter 10: Practicing Positive Mindfulness 83

Mindfulness... 83
Observation..84
Description 85
Participation 85

Tips on Practicing Mindfulness 86
Techniques and Exercises for Using Mindfulness in Your Life... 87
Meditation 87
Guided Meditation Through Audio Recordings...........88
Do the Raisin Exercise 88
Mindful Observation...89
Mindful Listening 89

Self-Compassion Break 89
Hold-and-Stretch Exercise 90
Five-Senses Exercise 90
Three-Minute Breathing Technique 90
Practice Mindful Eating 90
Think About Your Thinking 91
Mindfulness Technique for Anger Management 91
Stare at a Circle and Reflect on It for a Minute or Two 92

Case Study 92

Conclusion 93

Chapter 11: Learning How to Regulate Emotions 94

Why Do We Use Emotion Regulation? 94

What are Emotions? 94

About Emotional Regulation 96

What is Emotional Dysregulation? 96

Strategies and Techniques to Use in Regulating Emotions 97

Case Study 102

Conclusion 103

Chapter 12: Developing Interpersonal Effectiveness 105

Goals of Interpersonal Skills in DBT 107

Activities That Might Improve Your Interpersonal Skills 108
1. Try Not to Listen 109
2. Sabotage Game 112
3. Count the Squares 112

7

    4. Non-Verbal Introductions 112
  Effective Communication............................. 113
  Conclusion... 113
Chapter 13: Practicing Distress Tolerance 115
  Creating Distractions 115
  Self-Soothing 116
  Improving the Moment 117
  Focusing on Cue-Controlled Relaxation 118
  Rediscovering Values 119
  Living in and Affirming the Moment 119
  Review the Four Modules of DBP 120
  Final Thoughts 121
Bibliography 124

Introduction

This book is entitled *Cognitive and Dialectical Behavior Therapy: Overcome Anxiety and Depression, Tackle Negative Thought Patterns, Control Your Emotions, and Change Your Mood Through Effective Psychotherapy*. It can serve as a guide to the future of living and coping with mental illness using two types of psychotherapy, cognitive behavior therapy (CBT) and dialectical behavior therapy (DBT). While there have been many people who have tried to destigmatize mental disorder, it remains a stumbling block for people in this world. They live and fight the illness, often alone and without any means of support. Perhaps you or a loved one may even be suffering from bouts of depression or anxiety. Everyone does, but some have more severe problems than others. That's why there are mental health professionals who are seeking to help those in need of a true solution for these kinds of issues.

Now, there has never been a better time to look for a treatment for mental health disorders. The topic has started to become something that people do not mind opening up about. You see celebrities who have revealed their struggle with bipolar disorder or other illnesses. It is no longer a concept that you have to keep secret. You shouldn't feel ashamed about it because it is merely a challenge that you need to face, albeit not on your own.

As mentioned above, two treatments are available for individuals who are suffering from illnesses, such as bipolar disorder, borderline personality disorder, depression, and anxiety disorders, among others. The first one is cognitive behavioral therapy, which focuses on helping the patients deal with their thoughts at the moment and aims to teach them how to react positively. The second option is dialectical behavior therapy, which is a special kind of CBT that trains the mentally troubled individuals to simmer down when their emotions become extreme.

CBT is a term that encompasses the different types of talk therapies that are currently in use to treat mental health conditions.[1] This form of psychotherapy remedies the emotional reactions of people to different situations, and its duration is supposed to last for only a short period. If symptoms of the disorder continue, a person may take other forms of talk therapy.

CBT emphasizes a positive and constructive therapist-patient relationship. It will work in the best way if there is trust between the patient and the therapist. The former needs to show their ability to use logic in different situations, after all, while the latter needs to encourage the client to practice solving in-depth reaction-related problems to avoid a more emotional and potentially destructive response. Since cognitive behavior therapy is a personal experience, a patient should not stick with a mental health professional that they cannot work well with.

DBT, on the other hand, is a form of CBT that helps people deal with pain and discomfort in their lives, as well as cope with complex and intense emotions that may cause them to act out in self-mutilating or suicidal ways. Whereas the technique highlights the importance of surviving with difficult thought patterns, it focuses more on how the

---

[1] 4 differences between CBT and DBT and how to tell which is right for you. (2017). Retrieved from
https://www.skylandtrail.org/About/Blog/ctl/ArticleView/mid/567/articleId/6747/4-Differences-Between-CBT-and-DBT-and-How-to-Tell-Which-is-Right-for-You

patient can develop coping mechanisms and strategies that will allow them to handle triggering factors more effortlessly in the future.

In this book, we will talk about the similarities and differences between CBT and DBT and describe the various techniques used by each form of talk therapy. There are many tips and tricks that we want to give you to help you find the right treatment in this process. However, it is important to note that this guide is not meant to be a substitute for professional mental health treatment. You may treat the book as an introduction to the two vital forms of psychotherapy that may increase your interest in understanding such alternative remedies. We recommend that you use this information as well to educate yourself about the distinctive points of the said treatments and evaluate whether you would like to start a treatment plan with your therapist soon.

If you are struggling with depression, anxiety or other burdensome issues, you should seek psychological help. It is not something that you should do alone. In truth, you do not deserve to feel isolated in this situation because all of us are meant to help each other. Therefore, it is crucial that you find the proper mental health assistance that you need to learn how to thrive with or get rid of your condition. We aim to describe how DBT and CBT, in particular, may be of help to you, but we still recommend that you see a therapist to learn more about what you can do to be able to recover from and manage your problems. If you are having suicidal thoughts, call **1-800-273-8255, the National Suicide hotline, to talk to someone who can help you.**

Finally, we want you to get the treatment that you need to deal with your mental illness effectively. Too many people refuse to seek therapy because they are either ashamed of what others might think of their decision or worried that they will become outcasts in society. However, by consulting a professional, you can get assisted by a psychologist or psychiatrist who has experience in helping people take control of their life once more. Isn't getting your peace of mind more vital than caring about the comments from the rests? Do what you need to do to feel well. Your health is of paramount importance; that's why you should prioritize yourself before others'. We hope that all of the information that you will find in this book can direct you towards the road to recovery.

Come with us on this journey of discovery in the world of CBT and DBT and learn how these treatments can help you live a better life.

Chapter 1: Understanding CBT

Cognitive-behavioral therapy (CBT) is a type of treatment that deals with a broad range of mental health problems. It is a form of psychotherapy used by counselors and therapists to treat individuals suffering from depression, anxiety, social anxiety problems, and obsessive-compulsive disorder, among others. According to Fenn and Byrne (2013), CBT explores the links between thoughts, emotions, and behavior.[2] It provides a directive, time-limited, and structured approach to support patients who have a variety of conditions. In addition to that, it offers stress relief to people and is the most researched and proven method of psychotherapy.

Basics of CBT

CBT is a method based on the cognitive model of mental illness developed by Aaron Beck, an American psychiatrist, in 1964 (Fenn & Byrne, 2013). As such, individuals are influenced by how they perceive certain situations based on their emotions and behaviors. However, how a person feels about an incident depends on their perception of reality rather than the actual situation itself. For example, a depressed fellow might have a different view of reality, which is negative, because of how he or she is feeling at a given time.

To understand the basics of CBT, it is essential to begin with a concept of how cognition works and how people think.

---

[2] Fenn, K., & Byrne, M. (2013). The key principles of cognitive behavioural therapy. InnovAiT, 6(9), 579–585. https://doi.org/10.1177/1755738012471029

Beck (1976) outlined three levels of cognition: (1) core beliefs, (2) dysfunctional assumptions, and (3) negative automatic thoughts. [3]

1. Core Beliefs

A person's core beliefs refer to the deep-seated beliefs that he or she has about self, others, and the world. They are acquired early on and influence an individual's childhood, adolescence, and later stages of life. Core beliefs are informed by the worldview that a person develops as he or she grows up and learns from his or her parents and surroundings. Such ideas include religion, the perception of work and play, the importance of studies, and the philosophy of relationships. Other core beliefs are influenced by how a person thinks or feels about the world based on socio-economic factors, as well as family relationships. Also, an individual's thinking can be affected by the kind of child he or she is in a family. For example, the firstborn might have a different perception of the world from the middle or youngest child.

2. Dysfunctional Assumptions

Dysfunctional assumptions are thoughts that a person develops based on "rigid, conditional rules for living that people adopt (Fenn & Byrne, 2013, p. 579)." These beliefs have evolved due to environmental factors, but they can also develop internally. Given the cultural and societal background of an individual, he or she may come up with specific ideas about how the world operates based on this experience which may or may not be true.

---

[3] Beck, A. T. (1976). *Cognitive therapy and the emotional disorders*. New York: Penguin.

3. Negative Automatic Thoughts (NAT)

Thirdly, a person may develop negative automatic thoughts (NAT) that originate from a combination of preceding factors. These thoughts arise without his or her prior knowledge about the subject and typically appear in people who are depressed or anxious. Therefore, the ideas are present within folks who got diagnosed with anxiety and depressive disorders.

Aims of CBT

The purpose of CBT is to teach patients how to be their own therapist (Fenn & Byrne, 2013, p. 580). By being able to identify and counteract a person's feelings, he or she can understand his or her own thinking and behavioral pattern. Thus, cognitive behavior therapy allows someone to stop relying on another person, who is highly skilled in counseling, to become a more independent individual living a more satisfied and comfortable life.

CBT depends on a collaborative process between a patient and a therapist. It is problem-directed with an emphasis on the present situation of a person. CBT also focuses on the "here and now" problems and difficulties. Instead of looking at what causes an issue, it looks at how a patient can change his or her state of mind regarding a situation.

With its emphasis on changing someone's way of thinking, it is easy to deduce that cognitive behavior therapy is goal-oriented. Each session has multiple objectives to achieve, and each target is defined by the SMART acronym. In other words, every goal is specific, measurable, achievable, realistic, and time-limited. For instance, a woman with OCD goes to therapy. This patient might spend three hours a day cleaning her room, and so her goal by the end of the CBT program is to spend only one hour daily on the said task.

Techniques and Methods Used

The standard treatment for cognitive-behavioral therapy lasts for five to 20 sessions with the supervision of a therapist. Hence, it is a short-term and goal-directed program. However, the counseling may be extended depending on the condition of the patient. In CBT, to be specific, the goal is to change how a person thinks. Therefore, it uses both cognitive and behavioral therapy techniques.

A crucial part of CBT is the concept of guided discovery.[4] In this method, the mental health professional wants to try to see the patient's view of things and help him or her become aware of his or her thoughts about a given situation. A vital aspect of this concept is the Socratic method of question and answer, which is based on the teachings of the ancient Greek philosopher, Socrates. He helped his students reach a conclusion without actually telling them the answer to a question. Using the same technique, the therapists probe into an individual's former assumptions and reasoning to question their thinking patterns and pieces of evidence of what they believe in. Then, they ask the patient if he or she trusts in those beliefs. Guided discovery is an essential part

---

[4] Padesky, C. (1993). Socratic questioning: changing minds or guiding discovery? Keynote address delivered at European Association for Behavioural and Cognitive Psychotherapies Conference, London, UK. Retrieved from https://padesky.com/newpad/wp-content/uploads/2012/11/socquest.pdf

of reaching a different level of cognition (Fenn & Byrne, 2013, p. 581).

Psychotherapists work with someone by planning each activity in a person's life. The two join forces to reduce the tasks that the latter has to deal with to a manageable number in hopes of eliminating the need to make more critical decisions. By organizing an individual's choices and thoughts, he or she can avoid procrastination and anxiety-causing situations.

Furthermore, the therapist gives the patient a daily set of routines and pleasurable activities to follow through. The former may also conduct behavioral experiments for people with anxiety disorders. With this technique, the mental health professional tests out potential disaster scenarios on a patient. This person has to walk through the different predictions of parts of a task. Over time, disastrous thoughts are studied and evaluated by the patient. If he or she refuses to go on public transportation because they think an accident might occur, for instance, it entails that the person believes that, by avoiding public transit, he or she can escape a dangerous situation. In this case, the therapist may work with the patient to quell the triggers of his or her anxiety to reduce negative thought patterns.

In addition to these techniques, progressive relaxation training and breathing exercises are incorporated to diminish the anxiety level of an individual. By thinking about how one should breathe and react to given stimuli, the person can train himself or herself to respond constructively and reduce anxiety.

CBT is a cost-effective form of therapy that can outweigh the costs of having to take medication over time (Dobson et al., 2008). Mindfulness-based CBT can prove to be beneficial to patients as well.

Finally, CBT is used to treat a variety of conditions, including depression, anxiety disorder, panic disorder, obsessive-compulsive disorder (OCD), and post-traumatic stress disorder (PTSD).

Chapter 2: Understanding and Identifying Issues That Arise in Everyday Life

In this chapter, we will explore various issues that arise in our lives, e.g., anxiety and depression, and find out how CBT can smooth out such concerns.

Within the cognitive-behavioral therapy program, patients with different mental health issues seek counseling from a psychiatrist, psychologist or therapist, who can help them achieve their treatment goals. Depression and anxiety are the two main conditions that a person may require psychological assistance for. Thus, we will describe the characteristics of these mental health problems, as well as their symptoms and treatment options.

We all have troubles in our everyday life. Different worries, fears, and frustrations mix with our daily routine. The same ideas go for "normal" people and those who have anxiety and mood disorders. After all, it is typical to feel stressed about moving to a new location, taking on a new job, tackling multiple tasks, and turning in a project on time for a deadline. Without a fair amount of stress, we might not be able to function normally and carry out day-to-day activities. Nevertheless, dealing with an unhealthy amount of anxiety and stress can cause deeper issues that need to be treated with psychotherapy and potentially medication.

If a person finds his or her everyday activities irrationally dreadful, he or she may experience a disabling feeling or paralysis. That can severely impact anyone's regular functioning. Whenever an individual's worries affect the ability to do simple tasks, he or she may have an anxiety disorder. This condition should be taken seriously because it can be just as challenging and in need of immediate treatment as heart disease or diabetes.[5]

The related conditions of anxiety include generalized anxiety disorder (GAD), panic disorder and panic attacks, agoraphobia, social anxiety disorder, separation anxiety, selective mutism, and specific phobias. Also, there are other disorders associated with it, such as obsessive-compulsive disorder (OCD) and post-traumatic stress disorder (PTSD).

According to the 2017 report of the World Health Organization (WHO), there were 264 million diagnosed with anxiety disorders around the world in 2015. Based on a poll conducted by the American Psychiatric Association (2018), anxiety disorders affect about 40 million people in the US or 18% of the population. They occur in 8% of children and teenagers, with most cases developing before the age of 21. Unfortunately, in spite of the widely available treatment options, more than a third of the population is suffering from anxiety disorders receive treatment. With the mental health stigmas and issues, though, it is quite difficult for people to remove their pride and get the help they need.

What is Anxiety?

According to the various sources from www.anxiety.org, anxiety-related illnesses include the presence of fear or

---

[5] Anxiety and Depression Association of America. (n.d.). Understanding the facts of anxiety disorders. Retrieved from https://adaa.org/understanding-anxiety

worry that does not go away and gets worse with time.[6] The disorder interferes with school or work life; fear and stress are normal feelings that come with significant stressors. However, if someone has anxiety, he or she will not leave home for an extended time out of fear of being in the middle of a crowd. This person will be unusually worried or nervous, and these pervasive feelings will interfere with his or her ability to function normally. With professional and clinical help, the patient will need to try to identify the cause of anxiety and assess whether its symptoms are proportional to it. If a person has the constant worry that takes over his life, then he or she may need to receive the proper treatment for the condition.

There are different kinds of anxiety disorders to note, including obsessive-compulsive and related disorders, trauma, and stressor-related disorders). Such conditions feature an excessive fear of perceived or real threats and exaggerate the possibility of disastrous scenarios. As a result, the patient will experience disturbances in his or her daily life.[7]

In addition to anxiety disorders, there is a panic disorder. A patient with the latter illness may deal with different symptoms over time, such as racing heartbeat, feeling of weakness, faintness or light-headedness, dizziness, and sweating. These signs manifest during a panic attack, which can be caused by a variety of stressors and reactions to stimuli. Panic attacks can last anywhere from ten minutes to an hour or longer, and they recur as a part of a patient's

---

[6] van Rooij, S. & Stenson, A. (n.d.). An introduction to anxiety. Retrieved from https://www.anxiety.org/what-is-anxiety

[7] Powers Lott, A. & Stenson, A. (n.d.). Types of anxiety. Retrieved from https://www.anxiety.org/what-is-anxiety

condition.

Another kind of disorder is separation anxiety. This form of anxiety is common in children and adolescents, but it can also be present in adults. The patient continually worries about losing a significant attachment figure, such as a parent or loved one. The person is also concerned that something traumatic might happen to his or her lover, friends or family and may fear to go to school or to leave the people who are special to him or her. With feelings, someone may experience symptoms like headache, nausea or vomiting when separated from loved ones (Powers Lott & Stenson, n.d.).

Anxiety that involves the fear of many people is known as agoraphobia. A person who has this condition will have a pathological fear of many things, e.g., using public transportation, being in big, open spaces, staying in enclosed areas, getting surrounded by big crowds, or even being outside of the home alone. Agoraphobia affects many people each year and causes a great deal of stress for an individual. It can also be something that shy people can have difficulty with (Powers Lott & Stenson, n.d.).

Finally, there is generalized anxiety disorder, which entails that someone worries about various things uncontrollably. It leads to feelings of restlessness or fatigue, lack of concentration, irritability or inability to falling or staying asleep. This, too, affects a lot of individuals.

People with anxiety disorders struggle with doing necessary activities. With the serious worries in their lives, they consider even the most minute details to contribute to significant events. And often, these folks imagine worst-case scenarios with catastrophic possibilities. For example, someone refuses to go outside where there is a thunderstorm for fear of getting struck by lightning. Or, a person might not want to drive for fear of causing or getting into an accident.

Anxious individuals deal with a variety of phobias that contribute to their condition and inhibit their ability to do the things that they enjoy the most. Because many people do not take them seriously like one would diabetes or another physical condition, millions suffer quietly, which leads to many complications. Men, to be specific, are reluctant to seek help for such a disorder. Likewise, women feel shame at admitting that they struggle with anxiety.

Depression

The other kind of condition that affects millions of people in the world is depression. It is a common but severe mood disorder that can severely impact how a person feels, thinks or acts in a given situation, as well as his or her sleeping, eating, and working habits. With a depressive condition, symptoms can last for at least two weeks. The types of depression include persistent depressive disorder, which lasts at least two years, postpartum depression (for women who have had childbirth), seasonal affective disorder, which happens with the changes of the seasons, and bipolar disorder, which is characterized by a series of extreme highs and lows.[8]

According to the National Institute of Mental Health (2018), if a person is depressed, he or she may feel persistently sad, anxious, or empty. Irritability can also be

---

[8] National Institute of Mental Health. (n.d.). Depression. Retrieved from https://www.nimh.nih.gov/health/topics/depression/index.shtml

a sign of depression, as well as deep feelings of guilt, worthlessness or helplessness. With such emotions, one may experience a decrease in energy level and fatigue even when doing tasks slowly.

Additionally, a depressed individual may become restless or unable to sit still. He or she may also have changes in sleep patterns and develop problems with sleeping at night or waking up very early in the morning. With the increasing stress levels, the patient will notice changes in appetite by either eating too much or too little as well. The most extreme cases may deal with thoughts of death and lead to suicide attempts (Depression, 2018).

Depression affects many people. Almost everyone knows someone who struggles with this mental disorder, considering it is a widespread phenomenon. As one of the most common mental health conditions, it has also received a lot of stigmas over the years. Consequently, many people have not been able to stand up and face the challenges that it comes with. As we have seen, many actors lost their lives in the depths of depression, including Robin Williams. Treatment for this problem is essential to the wellbeing of the people who got diagnosed with it. This condition affects people of any age, but it often begins in adulthood. Depressive episodes can occur in children and adolescents, too, but in a low mood.

Principles of Automatic Intrusive Thoughts

Within anxiety and depression, some symptoms indicate the presence of negative thought patterns, which can lead to a downward spiral. Klinger (1978, 1996) has proven in his studies that the average duration of a specific thought is five seconds and that a person may have up to 4,000 different ideas every day.[9] There is also a type of thought that may enter someone's mind, which may not be helpful. It is called automatic intrusive thought.

David Clark defines unwanted, intrusive thoughts to be any distinct, identifiable cognitive event that is unwanted, unintended and recurrent.[10] These thoughts interrupt a person's ability to concentrate and perform day-to-day tasks. They have a negative impact on one's health as well. Another researcher, Rachman (1981) has said that unwanted ideas are "repetitive thoughts, images, or impulses that are unacceptable and/or unwanted…and are accompanied by subjective discomfort.[11] These intrusive thoughts may appear out of the blue in various forms such as daydreams, nighttime dreams, and fantasies, as Singer (1998) has indicated in his study. [12]

Properties of Automatic Intrusive Thoughts

---

[9] Klinger, E. (1978–1979). Dimensions of thought and imagery in normal waking states. Journal of Altered States of Consciousness, 4, 97–113.

Klinger E. (1996). "Emotional influences on cognitive processing, with implications for theories of both," in *The Psychology of Action: Linking Cognition and Motivation to Behavior* eds Gollwitzer P., Bargh J. A., editors. New York: Guilford Press, p. 168–189.

[10] Clark, D. A. (2005). Intrusive thoughts in clinical disorders: Theory, research, and treatment. Guilford Publications.

[11] Rachman, S. (1981). Part 1. Unwanted, intrusive cognitions. Advances in behaviour research and therapy, 3, 89–99.

[12] Singer, J. (1998). Daydreams, the stream of consciousness, and self-representation. In R. Bornstein & L. Masling (Eds.), Empirical perspectives on the psychoanalytic unconscious. Empirical studies of psychoanalytic theories (Vol. 7, pp. 141–186). Washington, DC: American Psychological Association.

There are distinct properties of automatic intrusive thoughts that should be considered. They occur in and originate from a person's consciousness. They are considered unacceptable and unwanted. Also, such thoughts interfere with someone's ability to function cognitively and undertake different activities.

Automatic intrusive thoughts are unintended ideas that tend to recur over time repetitively. An individual who is caught up in one will find that it easily captures his or her attention and distracts him or her from daily activities. As a result, adverse effects become very difficult to control (Clark, 2005). As these thoughts are spontaneous, people can have a hard time avoiding thinking about these mental intrusions as well.

Research suggests that intrusive thoughts are present mostly in individuals who struggle with worries, doubts, and anxiety disorders. For example, one study from Klinger & Cox (1987-1988) found that 98% of participants thought that intrusive thoughts were related to their everyday experiences. [13] The content of this investigation relates to how people think when they are awake and what kinds of experiences they have when daydreaming and being lost in thought. Participants had beepers, and they recorded what they were thinking throughout the day. It was important to help people see what thoughts they were contemplating in various situations.

Origin of Unwanted Thoughts

There is not enough empirical research to talk about the

---

[13] Klinger, E., & Cox, W. M. (1987–1988). Dimensions of thought flow in daily life. Imagination, cognition and personality, 7, 105–128.

origin of unwanted and intrusive thoughts. However, Salkovkis (1988) has spoken about the fact that unwanted thoughts are a part of a human's natural inclination to do problem-solving and brainstorming.[14] Therefore, undesirable mental intrusions can help a person solve complex issues and have positive and negative intrusions.

Unwanted thoughts are inevitably in someone's genetic makeup. There's not much you can do to stop them from occurring, especially as they tend to recur over time. On the other hand, a person can react to the situation in a constructive way. People who have anxiety disorders, to be precise, tend to have more of this kind of thinking because of the nature of the problem. It is a treatable condition that may require medication, but CBT likewise is a good complementary treatment.

The Thought-Feeling-Action Connection

When looking at how an individual deal with his or her feelings, it is important to note how he or she responds to different thought processes. With the CBT model, one can see that ideas relate to our feelings and how we behave. It is useful to try to chart out how a person feels every day by choosing to pause and reflect at least three times a day. That's only when one can understand someone's thoughts. Here are a few examples of how an individual's ideas connect to his or her feelings and actions.

Example 1

---

[14] Salkovskis, P. M. (1988). Intrusive thoughts and obsessional disorders. In D. Glasgow & N. Eisenberg (Eds.), Current issues in clinical psychology (Vol. 4). London: Gower.

Situation: Friday night

Thinking: I am all alone, and everyone on my Facebook feed is out for dinner with friends.

Feeling: Sadness and depression

Action: Stay in bed all evening and watch Netflix. Not pick up the phone to message a friend.

Example 2

Situation: Got a good grade on a test

Thinking: Wow! I'm so smart. I got an A!

Feeling: Excited! Happy!

Action: Go and celebrate the achievement with friends

With these preceding examples, it is clear that thought leads to a feeling that causes someone to act. It can be done in either a positive or negative way, depending on the emotion or thought that a person has. Nevertheless, the principle is the same. A thought or feeling demands a response, and that can be carried out either constructively or destructively. It is essential for people, therefore, to become mindful of how he or she deals with their complicated feelings because they can be overpowering and influence one's way of thinking and behavior. By understanding how it all relates together, a person can achieve positive results.

Chapter 3: Getting Your Life Back: Proven CBT Techniques

In this chapter, we will talk about proven CBT techniques that are used today.

The essence of cognitive behavior therapy is to change a person's way of thinking so that he or she can deal with different situations. The means of achieving success in this pursuit depend on how much thought and careful planning the individual does. If someone is a careful planner, after all, he or she will succeed in his or her endeavors. The first step in this process is to set realistic targets and objectives for your treatment plan.

Set a Goal

When you think about what you want to do with your life, think about things that you want to modify instead. Come up with some small, short-term goals that you can do within a short period, as well as medium- and long-term objectives that you want to accomplish in this lifetime. You can set goals for different aspects, including school and work, relationships, finances, lifestyle, health, and fitness, among others.

The objectives that you set should be unique and attainable. You need to be sure that they are realistic and achievable. If you set goals that are too high, you will lose motivation and get discouraged because you cannot attain them. For example, if you have never gone to the pool, expecting that you can go there for one hour, five times a week, is unrealistic. That may be your long-term goal. However, in case you want to improve with your fitness level, you will need to start small.

Next, goals need to be concrete and specific. You will be able to quickly achieve them once you define what they are clearly. If you are too vague with your expectations, you will not be able to make progress with your endeavor. However, if you are specific with your goal, you can set targets at each phase of the journey and check off what you've already done. You can then monitor your progress and move forward one step at a time.

For example, "read more" is not a concrete goal. What do you want to read? How long do you want to read? How many books would you like to go through during the day or week? To make this objective more specific, you need to add the number of books that you want to focus on, for how long, and when you aim to begin reading. You may also say that you want to do it for two hours every day and finish two books per month.

Let's now look at some more vague and concrete goal examples.

Vague Examples of Goals	Specific Examples of Goals
Eat more healthy foods.	Eat a banana for breakfast.
Socialize more.	Sign up for a foreign language conversation group and meet other language learners.
Be less nervous.	

Travel more.	Practice meditation and prayer.
Work out more.	Take a trip to NYC for my 35th birthday.
Cut out social media.	
	Go to the gym for 30 minutes a day for three sessions per week.
Spend less money.	
	Delete my Facebook and Instagram accounts and spend more time with family.
	Set a specific budget that you follow each month.

The next thing you need to do is to break your goal into different achievable and meaningful steps. Say, your objective is to make more friends at school. An initial goal, therefore, is to ask a classmate or seatmate to join you for coffee one day. If you want to find a new job, a smaller goal is to apply for two jobs in one day and send out a resume for the position that you're interested in.

After this step, you need to identify hindrances that might

prevent you from achieving your goals. For instance, one obstacle to being able to cut out social media is the fact that all your friends use the same channels, and you are afraid of missing out on the important events that they post on their accounts. You can resolve this issue by finding other ways to communicate with your friends other than social media.

Once you have identified potential hindrances, you should write down your goals in a planner or notebook. You should schedule all your activities on different days of the week as well. Although it is helpful to have a planner, you should not stick to it religiously. You should make time for unpredictable situations that may delay or postpone your plans. That's why it's important always to have a plan B just in case something happens.

If you have accomplished your goal, you should reward yourself. It's vital to give yourself some merit for your endeavors. Say, buy a book for yourself, get movie tickets, et cetera. You can also have a relaxing evening out afterward. Finally, don't forget how important it is to give yourself positive affirmations. E.g., "I finished it!" or "Yay! I did so well!"

If you were unable to accomplish your goal, re-evaluate why you failed to do it. Try to make sure that the objectives are achievable and concrete. Rework the process that you took again so that you will be able to achieve them next time.

Evaluate Your Goals

In deciding what kind of goal you want to pursue, you have to determine whether a target is actually yours. For many children, their parents are the ones who come up with objective, and the kids are merely expected to follow their wishes. It makes the youngsters miserable, and they often have to go through their lives pursuing their parents' dreams. This case is especially true with Asian parents. For instance, think of a Korean mother who wants her daughter to grow up and learn how to play the violin well. We all know people who are like this. With parents continually pressuring their children to do well with their studies, they can also put on a goal that the child ultimately does not want. If the mother or father wishes for the child to go to Harvard, the youngster has to comply or be labeled as a rebel. It is not a healthy dynamic, in any case.

Therefore, it is crucial to find and follow your dream, not someone else's vision for your life. Your goal does not have to come from others. Do not let someone else rule over you and influence your objectives. You must take ownership of your dreams and goals; after all, it is a uniquely individual thing. By doing so, you have more responsibility for your life, and it can help your situation improve drastically. Determining your dream will afford you many opportunities and chances to as a person as well - something that you might never find otherwise.

Deal with Your Pessimistic Thoughts

The crucial part of CBT is learning how to deal with those negative thoughts that pollute your mind. Because you have the goals to achieve success in life, you also need to find a way to bring your wellness plan to fruition. To make it happen, you ought to counteract all those negativities, take a side, and be more proactive in getting things together. The mind is like a battlefield, and you have to know how to play the game with it. The human brain is one of the most complicated things in the universe, and it matters to learn how to deal with the presence of negativity that can severely impact your overall outlook.

Thus, always keep your goals and dreams in mind. Think to yourself: "I am a capable person. I have been very successful in the past. I have a plan that I want to execute carefully and successfully. I can do it!" Giving yourself the emotional pep-talk will pump up your spirit and get you ready to achieve the objectives that you have set for yourself. Stay encouraging and affirm your abilities and what you have been able to accomplish as well. You can say, "I am super talented and smart. I am gifted in this area. They chose me for this job for a good reason. I know that I can do everything I set my mind to."

Also, it is essential to counter negativities by invalidating them. The truth is that feelings and thoughts can lie to you. They don't always accurately reveal the real situation that a person is in. Therefore, you need to find ways to say things like "That's a lie!", "It's not true!", and "Shut up!" You should voice out the lies that you feel. It is a good way to respond to these problematic thoughts.

Finally, countering negative ideas is about framing your mindset so that you no longer think about the pessimistic stuff in your life. In this manner, you will see the positive. Practicing a thankful attitude will help you to achieve the latter. Think about the things that make you grateful for what you have. E.g., home, shelter, spouse, kids, and all those other things. Gratitude can work wonders for your life and make you happier, especially when dealing with negative thoughts.

Conclusion

To sum up, it is important to look for something that drives you to pursue a goal. Finding a target can help you to achieve something in your wellness program. If you have one, then you will be able to go after it with all you have.

You should find goals that are reachable. They shouldn't be the types that are either too lofty or too high to achieve. Instead, they should be achievable within a reasonable timeframe.

Find a goal that meets your expectations and works in accordance with the dream for your life. It shouldn't be someone else's even if that person happens to be your parent, sibling or close relative. It needs to be yours. You should do it because you love it, not because another individual obligates you to do it.

Next, you need to evaluate how realistic your goal is. Think about the expectations you have of yourself, as well as how you can reach your goal. More importantly, you should learn how to counter the negative thoughts that may come into your mind along the way as you seek to live a meaningful and goal-driven life. Although you may face some challenges, you can still achieve the objectives that you have set for yourself. All things are possible in due time.

Strive to do your best, and you can succeed in meeting your expectations. Set the goal. Evaluate it. Achieve your objectives and milestone. Live your life in joy and fulfillment.

Chapter 4: Reshaping Your Attitude

In this chapter, we will discuss how CBT helps patients modify their attitude.

There is power in positivity that goes more than what meets the eye. You can indeed make a difference in your outlook when you look on the bright side of things. You will wake up in the morning on Monday thinking: "I can do this! I want to go to work today! It's going to be great!"

When you see that you can bring something good into this world, you will need to have a positive attitude and adjust your expectations. Think about it. Life is too short for you to go through it while complaining about every little detail. And we know that everyone likes to complain about the little things in life, such as a meal that is taking too long to be prepared in a restaurant, the noise that's happening during your coffee break or the temperature in your office. Although life is a bit of a downer sometimes, it does not always need to be like that. For this reason, we are going to look at how you can have a positive attitude and how it can change the way you approach new situations.

First, it is essential to realize that there are a lot of sources of difficulties and challenges in our lives. Nothing worth pursuing ever comes easily. It always takes hard work and dedication to accomplish even the most minute of tasks. And often, we cannot achieve our goals because we are discouraged under the weight of all the expectations that have been cast on our shoulders both by others and ourselves. In the midst of all of that, there is a need to pursue our goals and dreams. When we think about the end goal, then we know that we are always moving forward, one step closer to that milestone that will make a difference in our lives. Perhaps your goal is earning that extra $5,000 per year or putting aside money for your next vacation or becoming healthier and having a more positive outlook and overcoming your depression. Sometimes, the more straightforward goals are better because they can lead us to pursue the more involved ones.

Want to Be More Positive? Practice Gratitude

So, you might ask, "Tina, how do you get this positive mindset that is supposed to change my life?" Well, I can say that it is a lot easier for you to achieve that than you may think. What I want you to do right now is write down ten things that you are thankful for on a piece of paper. Get out a pen and notepad, and jot down all of your thoughts. Give yourself about five minutes to do this. You can see what influences your thoughts by getting a feel or what makes you thankful.

Gratitude is one of those powerful things. It helps you get out of the rut whenever you feel stuck. It makes you happier. It enables you to overcome the depressive blues. When you have a situation when you lose a job or have a catastrophic situation throw you a curveball, you may feel helpless and completely shattered from the damage that it has caused you. However, when you write down what you are thankful for, you will see how much blessed you are and have been given much in your life. The truth is, no one deserves this life. It is a gift - and a precious one at that. When you realize how much stuff has been handed to you, you should see that you have many people to thank for pulling you out of the gutter. Think of your parents, friends, financial situation (whether it's good or bad), community, job (not everyone has a good job these days), et cetera. Reflect on these blessings and take away the feelings of entitlement which you may be feeling about them. Realize that you get a lot more than what you deserve, and that is a gift of grace. Taking a moment to say thank you to someone who has made a difference in your life is an integral part of practicing gratitude. And, believe me, it will light up your whole day.

Stop for a Minute and Write Down Ten Things You are Thankful for and Then Come Back to Me

Once you have done that, you are on your way to becoming a more positive person. Remember a time when you were successful. In high school, you got an A on that English paper and ended up getting a good grade in the class. Or, in the university, you landed a premium internship for a consultancy firm that eventually led to a full-time job there. Perhaps you were able to overcome a severe disease that you got healed from miraculously. Be grateful and remember the times that went by and how you managed to get over many things. Think of how strong you are in surmounting any challenge that comes your way. Not everyone can fight as hard as you can. Having a mental illness can be hard. It can be so debilitatingly difficult to get out of bed in the morning. As soon as you have been able to overcome that difficulty, recognize it and celebrate it! It's the best way forward!

Become a Positive Hero

Having developed a positive mindset, you can now change the world. And one of the best ways to do so is to help others around you. That can alter your mood and feeling a lot more than anything. For example, when you help an elderly lady cross the street with her groceries, you do something special for someone else. That can boost your self-esteem and make you feel happy.

Helping is a form of therapy, which enables you to make a difference with others around you. It is very powerful. When you have a mindset of helpfulness and positivity, you can change a lot of things everywhere, as well as develop your mindset and attitude. For instance, if you smile at your reflection in the mirror and at others, you will find that you feel a lot better about yourself. It will allow you to feel much better about yourself. It allows you to enjoy that positive emotion.

This effect can be more powerful when you try laughing. Whether you crack a joke, watch a comedy on Netflix or laugh with your friends, laughter has been proven to be a great medicine to fight off the negative thoughts that may surround you. All of these things contribute to your positive feelings and enable you to feel excellent in the process. It is crucial to develop a mindset of playfulness, gladness, and thankfulness. This will make you a positive hero who can be a source of light amid the darkness of negativity in this world. As we have mentioned, there is much to be depressed about in this world; however, you can do your part to make the planet a better place by infusing your environment with positivity. That is going to change both your mindset and the world itself.

I am not going to lie to you; it is going to be hard to be positive at times. You might suffer a lot from the cares and worries of this life. Some days, you may wonder, "Why do I care? Why should I go to work today?" You may want to lay in bed all day and sleep because you cannot motivate yourself to keep going. But what if I were to tell you that it is possible to overcome your self-doubt by being a positive and more productive person? Indeed, it is possible.

Case Study

Jeremy was having a hard time in school. He flunked his math test and could not motivate himself to study for the test. The boy had a lot of worries and wondered if he would be able to get into college with a low grade in that class. He knew that he was naturally not good at math and started to get depressed. It got so severe that Jeremy was unable to get out of bed in the morning. So, he went to see his therapist who was teaching him some CBT techniques.

His name was Dr. Yellen, who happened to be a talented psychologist. Dr. Yellen told Jeremy that he needed to set a goal for himself to get out of that place of negativity. He wanted him to try for a C in the class at least and get some tutoring help in the process. Jeremy felt better and realized that this action plan was the best way forward. So, he worked with his tutor named Jack. Together, they worked everything out. Jack said to Jeremy, "I know that you're doing your best. You are trying hard, and you should not give up for anything. Tell yourself, 'I am a capable person. I can do it!'" Jack taught Jeremy a lot of positive self-talk, and this helped Jeremy a lot, especially when he was facing different challenges in his life.

Jeremy once got an "F" on his test. Instead of telling himself, "You're so stupid. Go home and cry on your bed," he said, "It's okay, Jeremy. You'll do better next time. Study harder, try harder, and you will do better. But you should seek help first." With this positive mindset, Jeremy learned to encourage himself and develop a "can-do" attitude. With the help of Jack, his tutor, he was able to successfully get that "C" in the math class after continuous encouragement and mentorship. It turned out great, and it was all because Jeremy was developing a positive way of thinking. There is so much power in optimism and how it can change your life. The fundamental principle in this example is that of positive self-talk. This is a way of coping with negative thoughts that inevitably infiltrate into our consciousness.

Conclusion

Be your positive hero and do that for others. That is a solution that is going to make a difference in this world. The way forward is to be the best person you can be, and that means playing on your strengths and developing your weaknesses. As we saw with the example above, Jeremy was able to get over his weakness by getting a "C" in his math class successfully. He did that with hard work and dedication but also with the help of his mentor and tutor, Jack. Together, they were able to accomplish the impossible, and it was amazing how it happened.

That is something you can achieve as well. Practice positive thinking, and you'll see the result of your hard labor and devotion. You have to work at re-shaping your attitude into something that you can do for yourself. It takes dedication and commitment and will involve your reshaping your mindset - that is true. However, when you give it your all, you will realize that everything is possible and that you can achieve your dreams when you set out to do so. When you believe in yourself, anything can happen. You can climb the highest mountain in the world, for one. You can get an "A" on the test that you have been dreading to take. You can achieve a Master's or even a doctoral degree. You can travel the world. You can be the person you were designed to be.

Believe in yourself and you will get to your dreams. Then, you can live a healthier, happier, and more meaningful life.

Chapter 5: Recognizing and Modifying Your Belief Systems

In this chapter, I will go into the basics of recognizing and modifying your core beliefs, which is essential for cognitive behavior therapy (CBT).

When you are depressed or anxious, your core belief systems are all out of whack, and you think that you cannot do anything about it. For example, you might feel that you are weak, needy, and incompetent, or as if you are someone who does not measure up to anything. You might tell yourself all these things to tear yourself down after a struggle that you have had. Or, you might feel that you are unlovable and different in the wrong way. You might also think that you are broken and that you have been burned many times by people. Worse, you might feel that you are a worthless person. All of these things encircle thoughts of negativity that you might have been dealing with for a while now.

You may feel helpless and cannot get out of this situation. You might have had these feelings for a long time. Often, people hold onto core beliefs that they have had since they were children, usually the kind that comes as the result of some traumatic incident or other things. These kids have possibly developed negative emotions over time, and it keeps coming back no matter how hard they try to get over it. And when you entertain an idea or try to ignore it, you can't get it out of your head. This is how negative thought patterns typically form.

Nevertheless, I am here to tell you that there is hope. You do not have to think about these ideas. You can divert or push them away from you. Here are some steps you can follow to do just that.

Step 1: Identify If Your Mentality Is Stable Or Changes With Your Moods

There are two kinds of negative core beliefs. One of them never changes. No matter what day it is, you know you are bad at science, so you feel bad and always beat yourself up about it. The other one is the type in which you can alter your mind depending on the circumstances. Say, you have had a perfect day at work. You feel as if you are on top of the world; that's why you go out to celebrate it. Then, you reinforce that feeling with self-talk, such as "I'm a pretty great person. I finished this project before the deadline, and I feel awesome!"

Now, let's say your shift has been horrible so far. A customer yells at you for a project that was handed in, and you think that you are a lousy worker and that you should quit your job. You might feel down in the dumps on that type of day. If you have the second type of mentality, though, you can turn your mood upside down. After all, just because you have a bad day doesn't mean you're an awful person. Bad days happen to everyone.

Step 2: Emphasize the Positive Thoughts That You Have About Yourself to Divert From Negative Ideas

By focusing more on the positive things that you can say about a circumstance, you will be able to get rid of those negative thoughts that lurk in your mind. However, that should not be your only end goal. You might not manage to eliminate the latter by enumerating the optimistic ideas alone because that's not how it works at times. You might have to still deal with a negative thought or two as they enter your life. What you can do is over-emphasize the positive to (hopefully) drown out the negative thoughts that encircle you. So, think of what's important and see the results of your labor.

Step 3: Start a Positive Thought Journal

For three weeks, commit yourself to jot down your thoughts and pieces of evidence to support your new core belief(s). For example, if you want to prove to yourself that you are a trustworthy and reliable person, you can write "I'm trustworthy" on a piece of paper and then mention all the reasons why you think so. Say, explain that you keep your appointments, maintain your commitments, stay true to your word, and always follow up with others. Write things like that each time it happens so that you have proof of how trustworthy you truly are. Don't beat yourself up if you make a mistake, though. You might fall flat on your rear end and make a blunder, but you can pick yourself up and say, "It was just a slip-up." This will make every difference as you seek to improve your situation.

Step 4: Re-Evaluate Yourself

In the next level, you should re-evaluate how you did. Perhaps you will notice that your core belief has changed from being overly negative (e.g., "I am not trustworthy" and "I am a liar") to being slight positive (e.g., "I am trustworthy and reliable"). It will take some time and practice, but once you achieve it, you will be so happy. Realize also that progress is to be had, although it takes time and commitment. Always make an effort to re-evaluate your efforts over time.

Step 5: Tell an Accountability Partner

The next step is essential because you cannot keep all these thoughts and ratings to yourself. You should tell a trusted friend or mentor about your goals so that they can hold you accountable for your thought patterns and encourage you as you try to improve. That person can be like a cheerleader to you who can share your struggles and victories. It is so helpful to have someone to remind you of your dreams and aid you through difficulties and challenges that you are sure to face in life.

Step 6: Try to Discover Where the Old Thoughts Came From

You should try to figure out where the negative thoughts are coming from so that you can understand why you feel the way you do. This also helps you to understand yourself a bit better. For instance, you might be an introvert, and you fear that other boys will make fun of you because of your lack of athleticism. Thus, you might have a trauma of doing sports-related activities with others and always make excuses to avoid them. A lot of these experiences originate from childhood and how we have dealt with awkward situations in the beginning. You should try to understand this because it will help you make sense of the negative thoughts that may permeate your mind at a given time.

Step 7: Watch Yourself Whenever You Spiral Into Negative Self-Talk

When you start to entertain negative thoughts (e.g., "I'm stupid") every time you forget your car keys or commit another mistake, you should talk to yourself in an encouraging way to be able to get back up again. Say something like, "We all make mistakes; it is okay. Don't worry about it." Give yourself space and time to recover from such incidents and keep going in your life.

Step 8: Evaluate How Much You Accept Negative Thoughts or Beliefs

Accepting or rejecting a negative thought or belief happens in the moment of thinking. And you have a choice: take it or ignore it and tell yourself, "That's a lie! Don't believe that!" You may experience a negative feeling at a given time, but that does not mean that you believe that point at all times. It may just be a passing phase that you experience sometimes. Take note of when this happens and act accordingly.

Let's look at a practical example of how this works. Julie is a student at Washington and Lee University. She is struggling to understand her history lecture and feels quite down about it. Julie continually tells herself, "I'm no good at history. I'll never pass this class. I'm a bad student." Lately, her grades have suffered. She had a traumatic accident and had to go to the hospital for two weeks. Her legs became disabled, and she was unable to walk.

Consequently, her negative self-talk amplified, and Julie began to berate herself for the situation that she was in. She could never give herself a break. Julie also had to ride a wheelchair into class every day and have people help her with her books and notes, et cetera. She struggled with self-pity and doubt and knew that she was weak at history, but Julie also wanted to succeed in school. Hence, she talked with her therapist about how her life could possibly improve and allow her to get better grades. Then, she spoke with her professor about how she could have accommodation for finishing her assignments with more time allowed. The professor, Dr. Hennings, was very understanding and wanted to provide everything she could to help Julie. In the end, Julie worked very hard. She never gave up. And she was able to get a passing grade in history class. Afterward, Julie said to herself, "See, you are not incompetent. You did it! You passed history class because you worked hard, and you are a dedicated person. You can do everything you set your mind to." When you apply this principle of positive self-talk on any aspect of your life, it will work wonders (as it did for Julie).

Conclusion

You can see the power of modifying your belief systems has helped many people like Julie to accomplish their goals. It is not always an easy feat to achieve, and a person may often feel a great deal of self-doubt and worry about how he or she will live his or her life. However, once you overcome the situation, everything becomes so much better, and your worry and doubt may disappear. You also begin to affirm yourself for all the positive things that you do well, and you do not stress over the ones that you don't. The difference that it will make in your life is incredible.

Chapter 6: Dealing with Worry and Anxiety

Everyone has worries. We worry about the weight we put on, how much money we have in our bank accounts, the mountain of bills that we get every month, and all the other things that we have to do in our lives. Although that is normal, for some people struggling with anxiety and depression, their worries severely impact their ability to function and perform daily activities. This is a significant hindrance that should be dealt with at once to prevent it from impeding someone's path to success.

In this chapter, therefore, we are going to explain practical ways on how to deal with the worries and anxieties that can easily overpower you.

Fight-or-Flight Response

When it comes to handling anxiety and worry, people tend to choose to either face the problem that is making them anxious or control the level of stress that they have to be able to solve the problem. Many individuals get tempted to avoid situations as well that will get them into trouble, and that puts them in an unfortunate situation. After all, if you try to avoid a stressful circumstance, the anxiety that you experience a second time will make the issue even more overpowering. Thus, it is best to figure out ways to respond to a given stressor instead of trying to get away from it.

One way to deal with your stress and anxiety is to engage in physical activities that will enable you to fight off your worries. Exercise has been a proven method to get rid of anxiety since you release endorphins and other feel-good chemicals when working out, which allow you to feel much better. Exercise also helps to reduce your nervousness.

Structured Problem-Solving

To be able to face your issues directly, you should rehearse a stressful situation beforehand and think of how you will react to it. This simulation will enable you to see how you should deal with a negative circumstance in the future. It will help you to know what you need to do to a problem as well. If you are usually a worrier, you will find that you can do better once you confront difficult matters with a practiced and structured way of solving an issue in advance.

Try to Limit Your Consumption of Technology and Messaging Tools

Technology has been a proven source of a lot of problems in our lives. No doubt, it is one of the main causes of anxiety because we check our Instagram or Facebook accounts constantly and see messages that make us worry. Technology has continually been a source of stress as well. If you deliberately limit your interactions with it, you will find just how freeing it is to do so. You will deal with fewer distractions and feel more productive overall. Try to spend a day with minimal use of technological advancements or none at all. You will see the difference in your outlook in life.

Try Meditation Techniques and Aromatherapy

When you are stressed at work or school and don't feel like there is a way out of it, you can try doing meditation. Find a quiet place to sit and relax with some good music that will give your mind a sense of calm. Close your eyes. Focus on your breathing. Practice mindfulness and enjoy a new way of thinking. You may also become more positive in the process, notice that your heart stops beating so fast, and be able to concentrate on essential matters. Furthermore, you can do aromatherapy by getting some candles or scented oils that will help you get back to where you need to be.

Take a Hot Bath/Shower to Try Aquatherapy

Another method that helps you is aquatherapy. Whenever you take a hot bath or shower, you instantly feel relaxed and refreshed. So, feel free to soak in the water longer than you usually do, allow it to exfoliate your skin, and notice the change in yourself.

Exercise

Although we have already mentioned the importance of exercising to improve your well-being, the best thing that you can do is find a type of activity that works for you. There are many options out there to try. Aerobics, in particular, is useful in releasing endorphins that help you feel good and boost your mood. You can experience both physical and psychological benefits when doing so.

Doing a lot of walking can also get your health in order. When you start feeling anxious or worried, you can take a long, brisk walk. Better yet, you can take a short, intensive jog around the block and feel the stress and anxiety go away. These steps will help you to experience freedom and peace of mind like never before.

Dealing with Procrastination

Procrastination is a problem that causes many people a lot of stress and anxiety. The reason why they struggle with it is that they don't know how to manage their time. Consequently, folks give themselves more concern than they need when they should only think of it like managing your money. You have to take it one step at a time; you can't have millions in the bank by merely praying for it. There are several steps that you should take to overcome procrastination.

1. Prioritize and do what absolutely must be done today. Then, focus on other tasks when you need to get them done.

2. Make a to-do list every day and check off much as you can.

3. Set daily goals for the tasks that you want to accomplish.

4. Set weekly targets that you wish to fulfill within a given timeframe.

5. Give yourself breaks from time to time. For example, some people go sabbatical and do no work on that particular day. This is a good way of managing stress and releasing the burden that can come from working for a whole week. Relieve yourself. Be gentle with yourself.

6. Reward yourself when things go well, too. Go to the movies, have a drink at the bar, and hang out with friends.

Procrastination is both a mindset and a habit that too many people are stuck with. However, you should not wait until it has taken over your life before you try to counter it. You can come up with an action plan now that will enable you to do all the things that you need to do each day. Then, you can reward yourself when everything goes well. Don't beat yourself up whenever things get busy, though, and you find yourself procrastinating on different tasks. It's normal; just go with the flow. You'll figure things out in time.

Conclusion

We have talked about the points of how to deal with anxiety and worry as they enter our lives. The best way is to try to minimize all causes of stress, such as procrastination. You may also limit technology usage and take a hot shower or bath, among other strategies that we have listed above. That's only when you will be able to live your life free of anxiety.

Chapter 7: Getting Rid of Negativity in Your Life

What is Negativity?

Negativity is a way of seeing the world that is usually marked by what a person feels about things, people or situations. It may not reflect reality, but some folks believe in it. The problem with negativity is that it is coming from deep within yourself. When you default to negative thinking, then you will only focus on the negative and not enough on the positive. This means a person may think of the worst possible thing that can happen in their life. Negative people are skeptical of advice that is given to them, and they tend not to trust people based on their past experiences.

Although someone may be negative, it is not a healthy mindset to get into, and it deeply hinders your ability to make connections with others. Are you the type of person to see the glass as half empty or half full? If you are optimistic about life, you will tend to focus on the latter. If you are a negative person, you will focus on the former and see the weaknesses in every situation or person.

When a pessimistic individual faces a challenge or difficulty, he or she will predict a negative result from it before the event even happens.

Where Do Negative Thoughts Come From?

Negative thoughts come from a variety of sources, such as patterns that we have formed over time and beliefs that we have made about the world. Values may include self-esteem, money, job, relationships, et cetera. To understand where the negative thoughts stem from, you have first to ask yourself some questions.

1. Do you always complain about every little thing?
2. Do you blame others before yourself?
3. Do you tend to predict the most unfavorable outcomes in a given situation?

Other things can also contribute to your negative thinking. E.g., criticizing people, feeling like you've been victimized by situations, having depressive thoughts, watching the news all the time and feeling bad about it, and always predicting disaster scenarios. As you consider such ideas, you have to realize that the more you hang out with negative people, the more pessimistic you will become. Negative thoughts spread like wildfire whenever you are in the company of folks who think that way. So, it's vital to find friends that can be encouraging and build you up instead of the ones who lead you towards the dark path.

Effects of Having Negative Thoughts

Negative thoughts severely impact your well-being. Whenever you have pessimistic ideas, your brain goes into survival mode and gets stressed about every situation that comes up. If a person experiences chronic stress, he or she will feel its effects physically and mentally. Whether or not you know it, you will see those negative thoughts hamper your ability to function and have long-term consequences. You may find that your appetite is suppressed as well or you might overeat at times to cope with the issues. After all, losing and gaining weight are common symptoms of dealing with negative thoughts because your body is experiencing stress a lot.

Additionally, negativities can cause you trouble with friends, colleagues, family, and others in your environment. As long as you dwell on the negative, other people will follow suit and be quick to judge and criticize the new folks that they meet. It creates a domino effect, which brings a great deal of stress and anxiety to everyone involved.

If you are always negative, you will notice that you get depressed a lot easier, too. You can never look on the bright side of life, and you do not trust anyone (including yourself). As a pessimist, you will be unhappy, and others will want to complain along with you. Being negative makes you a miserable person and prevents others from hanging out with you.

It is crucial to go through each day without negativity. It can cause a host of health problems and even affect the well-being of your loved ones. Moreover, if you are with people who bring you down, you will not want to be with them. Therefore, it is vital that you find people who are positive and can be a great influence to you.

Below are 31 ways to stop being pessimistic and start living a life that is full of joy and positivity.

1. Create distance between you and the negative people around you. Think about a person you know who is always negative and complains about every situation. If that is a friend or coworker, you should put some distance between you and him or her. Do not spend too much time together as much as possible; the more you do so, the more you might

experience hurt and anxiety.

2. Do not feel bad about cutting your ties with negative people. If you have to end relationships with them, merely think that you have to do what is right for you. Perhaps you have spent a long time with this person, but you can always find other people who can be encouraging to you. Try to prioritize the latter type of individuals.

3. Do not argue with negative people. Such arguments can lead to drama, and you do not want to intermingle with that. Instead, you should walk away from it and come back when everyone is ready to see reason.

4. Be with positive individuals. By focusing your energy on them, you will naturally become more positive as well. You will feel good around these people and have a more positive attitude as a result.

5. Do a sport or join a club activity. Hobbies and sports are great ways to infuse your life with positivity. When you are with other like-minded individuals, you can accomplish a lot of things together. This creates a positive vibe that you want to have.

6. Practice positive self-talk. This one is big. If you want to become positive, you are going to have to say positive things to yourself to build yourself up. Therefore, you should find a lot of positive affirmations that will increase your self-confidence and enable you to do something great. Think of saying things such as "You are awesome!" or "You are an amazing baseball player!" or "You do such

good work." If you practice giving yourself compliments, you will find more affirmation enter your heart, and things will be great.

7. Replace the negative thought with a positive thought. Instead of dwelling on former, try adding the latter when your thoughts start to swirl in the negative region. You will be amazed at the power of positive thinking and how it changes your whole day when you can do that. For example, you have a case of the Mondays, and you dread going to school or work on that particular day. Try replacing that thought with something positive, such as "I look forward to having my nice cup of coffee and walking into work and smiling." You will alter your whole outlook by doing so.

8. Notice when you are slipping into a negative thought pattern. You should watch yourself lest you fall into the trap of dwelling on the negative. For instance, you watch the news, and you see some horrendous event happens, such as a terrorist attack. At once, your mind goes to the negative and predicts that a disastrous scenario will happen.

9. Be conscientious and do it. The process of negating all those harmful thoughts is going to take a careful and diligent process that you will have to go through. You must have the intent to stop the negative thoughts from taking over your life.

10. Practice gratitude regularly. When you pause to think about the things that you are thankful for, you will have more positive energy that will naturally gravitate from you, and you will feel happier. Also,

you will be a more loving and caring person who wants to think of others and how they have benefited or helped you.

11. Think about every beautiful occurrence in your life. Life is filled with sorrow, heartbreak, and challenge, but you should also be reminded of all the good things, as well as be grateful for the experiences that you have had. After all, not everyone has the privileges that you have.

12. Write down at least five things that you are thankful for every morning. You can do it in a journal, a piece of toilet paper or even a table napkin. The writing material does not matter as long as you are writing down the things that make you grateful. You can start your day on a high note this way because you will infuse your whole system with positive energy.

13. Don't complain. Instead of complaining to get your way, stop! Hold the thought and move on. You should not do any complaining because the truth is that it does very little in helping you. Often, complaining will merely push you from what you want, so it's useless.

14. Tell someone "I love you." This could be a loved one or a close friend, guys and girls included. Telling someone that you love them is going to send a lot of positive feelings into your system because there is no group of words that is more sure to win your heart as "I love you."

15. Don't gossip in your office. Gossiping is contagious, and it infects workplaces and schools. It is not good;

in reality, it can genuinely cause strife and discord anywhere. You want to avoid it as much as you can.

16. Say "thank you." No matter how small the deed is that is done for you, it is always best to the person who gave you a favor. Practice saying it a lot because there is nothing like expressing gratitude to whomever you are speaking to. If someone does something nice for you, e.g., hold the door open, say "thank you." Expressing gratitude is an essential part of being happy.

17. Express your positive feelings. Another good thing to do is to express the optimistic emotions that you are experiencing with others. It lightens your mood and enables you to connect with others, which, in turn, fills the room with good vibes.

18. Do not try to read others' minds. A lot of times, we assume the worst in what people think about us. It is best to stop believing that the individuals around you merely have ill feelings towards you. This will only bring you more stress and anxiety. Therefore, you should stop jumping to conclusions and thinking negatively about how others view us. Just relax and keep calm.

19. Do not watch the news. There is nothing more depressing or unnerving than watching the headlines that appear on your TV screen. They make a killing off of the bad news that is making headlines every day. It is a big money-making scheme to get viewers to watch and tune in. However, you should not be always watching the news because that will only feed negative thoughts into your mind and

make you miserable. Instead, you should focus on a romantic comedy show or do more uplifting activities that will boost your happiness and sense of fulfillment.

20. Set daily achievable goals. Being a goal-driven person is an integral part of becoming a more positive person because you see how you can achieve everything that you set out to do each day. When you do this, you will be more joyful and successful. It will also make a difference in your self-esteem, confidence, and overall morale. And when you achieve your goals, go out and celebrate with a glass of wine or a pint of beer.

21. Do not multitask. Instead, do one thing at a time. If you want to be a successful person, one of the best things you that can do for yourself is to stop trying to do everything at once. This practice makes you more attention-deficit and causes you to complete tasks in a rush because you want to check them off your to-do list quickly. The truth, however, is that you get a lot more done when you are careful and focusing on a single activity since your brain is wired to concentrate on just one thing at a given time. Say, do yourself a favor and stop having so many tabs open on your Google Chrome browser. Stop responding to texts during your work hours as well.

22. Look for your higher calling in life. Another thing that you have to do is be mindful of your purpose on earth. For example, you might turn to religion or values and ethics to fulfill your calling. However, having a vocational purpose is going to make you a happier and more positive person because you live

into what makes you a productive human being and think about "Why am I here?" It helps you to philosophically analyze and see how you can make the world a better place, too.

23. Do not dwell on the past. Negative people tend to think a lot about their past failures and dwell on the pessimistic side of life. It is vital to stop doing that and focus on the positive things that you have done. Reflect on your amazing achievements; be proud of what you have been able to accomplish. Instead of thinking too much about your past or even reliving your history, you should strive to live in the present.

24. Do a lot and stay busy. The more work or activities that you do, the better you will feel. It is essential for you to manage your time well and stay active. Make to-do lists and stick to them, for instance, and stop wasting your time on things that are not going to help you in the long run.

25. Sleep well at night and take naps when you need to. This is quite crucial. You are going to need plenty of sleep to get you through each day. Hence, you should make an effort to sleep well at night and get the recovery that you can have after a long day.

26. Eat healthy foods. You should also strive to have a balanced diet that will allow you to remain positive and upbeat so that you will be able to tackle any challenge that might be thrown your way. Eat lots of fruits, vegetables, and proteins to make your diet healthy and fresh.

27. Get your dose of exercise. Working out is a powerful

way of enabling your body to release feel-good chemicals, e.g., endorphins. You should try to exercise at least five times a week, 45 minutes for each session. This will help you to be a bit more positive.

28. Do not spend too much time on social media. This is a big time waster, and it also produces a lot of stress and anxiety. If you are spending a lot of time on Facebook, you are likely comparing yourself with others, especially celebrities. It creates feelings of negativity and fear that you do not want to have. As a result, you should spend a lot less time on social media because it will only make you unhappy and miserable.

29. Keep your workspace and home neat and organized. When you keep your space orderly, you will feel a lot better about yourself and everything around you. Plus, there is nothing like a clean house to come home to, you know. Therefore, it is vital that you do this to lift up your mood.

30. Cut out things from your life that are not benefiting you, and say "no" to things that you do not need. It is important to do the latter, primarily if those activities can put you at risk. You should get rid of non-essential items as well that are tearing you and your relationships down. Only focus on the things that are going to build you up instead. This is a crucial part of living a healthier and more stress-free life.

Now that we have given you 30 tips on how you can remove the negativities in your life, we hope that you will take action and do them for real. Negative thoughts make you unhappy and miserable. It will take some time for you to get used to not complaining or focusing on the negative, but once you do, you will find that you are living a happier and more fulfilled life. Your existence will then seem more meaningful and purpose-driven, and that will improve your overall outlook in life. Let's now look at a case study of how this method works in reality.

Case Study

Jennifer used to be a very negative person. She was always complaining about the weather and the office culture that she was in. She had something to gripe about every day. Because of that, Jennifer became the talk of the town and was known as Ms. Negative Nancy to everyone. They tended to tease her about it as well, which offended her and made her cry at home on the weekends. Her negativity caused a great deal of anxiety and stress to Jennifer, and her blood pressure was going up several points every day. She knew that she needed the money to survive, although she hated her job. Yet, Jennifer did not want to admit that she had a negativity problem. She always thought that she could manage on her own and that she was overcoming her negativity. Despite that, Jennifer ended up spouting out insults at people and tried to lure them into her negativity circle so that she could have "good" company. Soon enough, the whole office was getting tired of it, and they started insulting each other and tearing each other down. It created a very hostile situation in which everyone was not having an excellent time at their workplace.

If we look at this example, we see that negativity breeds negativity. Whenever there is a bad apple, it spoils the whole lot of them. Jennifer was a Negative Nancy, and as such, she dealt badly with the people around her, thus creating a wall of hostility. Jennifer complained about every other matter in the office, and it was a contagious habit; that's why everyone around her started complaining as well. It was infectious in a bad way. Let's continue the story.

It got so bad that people were turning against each other and causing more strife, to the point that some employees got fired because of it. Jennifer also finally got fired because a group of her colleagues turned on her. When she got sacked, though, Negative Nancy immediately slipped into depression and had to go to her psychiatrist for help. She was on antidepressants for her seasonal depression.

Jennifer sought mental assistance from her psychiatrist, who was able to give her advice about what she should do. He listened about all the difficulties that she had been through and could tell that she was being quite negative. So, he proposed an idea to her and said, "Why don't you try to be positive for a day and see what happens?" Jennifer replied, "Why not?"

So, Negative Nancy tried to be positive for one day. She followed her doctor's advice on how to be optimistic, showed gratitude to others, and focused on all the blessings that she had in her life at the time. At the end of her first day, she still complained. But then, the next day, she realized how much she had to be thankful for and counted her immeasurable gifts.

Jennifer said, "I can't believe how lucky I am to be alive. I have a wonderful doctor and husband. I also have my children, who have comforted me through this tough time. What more could I ask for? I am blessed!" Then, she started to count her blessings every day. She didn't stop doing it because Jennifer felt that she could always say that she was better off than someone else. As a result, the pessimistic lady realized that she could be happy and content with all the little things that life gave to her. Eventually, Negative Nancy was seen smiling more often. She laughed a lot more and was able to get off her antidepressants after one month of trying her doctor's positivity method. It was infectious. Everyone around her saw just how much of a good life she was living and they wanted to live like her. In case you are wondering about her job situation, Jennifer was able to land an even better job with higher pay at a large corporation in a more developed city.

The moral of this story is that you need to be positive all the time. Drown out the negative voices in your head and do something amazing. Because Jennifer focused on what was positive, she was able to see a dramatic difference in her morale and her ability to relate to others. They wanted to be around her now rather than push her away, unlike in the case of her previous job. Jennifer also managed to overcome her depressive feelings and need for antidepressants, which had become her go-to solution for her problem. She could not get out of the slump and into a more positive and upbeat situation since Negative Nancy had been stuck in her cycles of negativity. Nevertheless, once she tried to be positive for one day, she was able to see immediate results and felt more thankful for the blessings that she got.

Conclusion

We hope that you have been able to realize how toxic negativity can be. It is something that needs to be avoided at all costs. Negativity can be detrimental to your physical and mental health. Often, it is difficult to silence the negative inner critic within you, but it is something that you have to learn how to do at some point. Cognitive-behavioral therapy enables you to silence that pessimistic voice in your head and allows you to live a life that is full of positivity. It is crucial that you find ways to look on the bright side to enliven your life and give you more joy and peace. Without an optimistic outlook, after all, it is hard to have a meaningful existence. Therefore, we highly recommend that you try to find things to be positive about and grateful for so that you do not have to spend your time and energy complaining about all the bad things that occured in the past. See the beauty of life and meditate on it. You'll feel an amazing difference afterward - that's for sure.

Chapter 8: The Emergence of Dialectical Behavioral Therapy (DBT)

Another type of treatment that is similar to cognitive-behavioral therapy (CBT) is known as dialectical behavioral therapy (DBT). The latter form of therapy was initially developed to treat patients with borderline personality disorder with the intention of reducing suicide risk and other self-harming behavior.[15] This treatment was quite helpful to adolescents who tend to engage in self-harm, e.g., burning and cutting. DBT emphasizes the use of "dialectics, the reconciliation of opposites in a continual process of synthesis," as cited in Marsha Linehan's research in 1993.[16] As it was originally supposed to help patients with suicidal tendencies, it has now been adapted for borderline personality patients, as well as other patients with serious mental health problems. It combines a therapy, which includes Eastern philosophy and teachings and highlights how the world moves with opposite ends of the spectrum, much like the yin and the yang (Linehan, 2001). [17]

DBT has a dialectic tension that involves the patient's acceptance of his or her condition and willingness to change

---

[15] Caplan, J. & Jellinek, M. S. (2009). Psychotherapy with children and adolescents. Developmental-Behavioral Pediatrics (Fourth Edition). Elsevier.

[16] Linehan, M. (1993). Cognitive-behavioral treatment of borderline personality disorder. New York: Guilford Press.

[17] Linehan, M. (2001). Dialectical behavioral therapy. Retrieved from https://www.sciencedirect.com/topics/nursing-and-health-professions/dialectical-behavior-therapy

his or her behavior. Thus, this technique consists of a lot of problem-solving methods and training that enable the person to adapt to new situations and experiences. One technique that is used is the mindfulness method, which allows an individual to live within the present moment and shut out everything that is distracting him or her within that moment.

DBT differs from CBT, in the sense that the latter integrates both cognitive and behavioral theories. [18] Dialectical behavioral theory, on the other hand, is based on Zen Buddhism, thus perpetuating a system of non-absolutes. Meaning, there is no single truth; that's why one has to work to integrate positive and negative perspectives within a person's life. The DBT model has been used to accomplish the following goals:

1. Reducing suicides and attempts to harm one's life
2. Treating individuals with trauma, including conditions like post-traumatic stress disorder (PTSD)
3. Enabling patients to find a higher calling or motivation to live
4. Helping individuals develop their self-esteem and sense of fulfillment

Origins of Dialectical Behavioral Therapy

Dr. Marsha Linehan was one of the first creators of DBT in

---

[18] Reddy, M. S. & Vijay, M. S. (2017). Empirical reality of dialectical behavioral therapy in borderline personality. *Indian Journal of Psychological Medicine, 39*(2), 105-108.

the 1980s. As the interest of the public became enthralled with borderline personality disorder (BPD), many people who thought that they had the condition were led to the office of mental health professionals. Linehan (1993) wrote that 11% and 19% of all psychiatric outpatients and inpatients, respectively, met the criteria for the disorder. At the time of writing her book on cognitive behavior therapy, Linehan indicated that there were inadequate treatments available to remedy the condition. She recognized how much treatment was needed to be provided to BPD patients, given that their cases were quite extreme, thus requiring the careful attention of a mental health provider. She also showed how borderline patients were quite numerous, and many doctors had to treat at least one of these patients (Linehan, 1993). These individuals demanded a lot of time and attention from the care provider, and so they could leave many mental health practitioners feeling overburdened from the lack of available resources. Linehan also revealed how many people had largely ignored the symptoms of BPD, such as self-mutilation and suicidal tendencies in her book.

The people who tend to injure or kill themselves tend to be women. Linehan (1993, p. 4) said that about 74% of the patients that have a borderline personality disorder (BPD) were women. The treatment that she proposed was a type of cognitive behavioral therapy, known as dialectical behavioral therapy (DBT), which was developed and used with women who had symptoms of BPD and also had previous histories of suicidal behaviors.

Although DBT originally was used to treat individuals with borderline personality disorder, it was eventually carried over to people with diverse mental health issues, including depression, bipolar disorder, eating disorders, and PTSD, among others.

Principles of DBT

DBT provides its patients with the ability to manage their overwhelming emotions, decrease their tendency to act out on their feelings without thinking, and reduce interpersonal and relational conflicts. Dialectical behavioral therapy focuses on giving a troubled individual the skills that he or she needs to deal with four key areas.[19] First, it uses mindfulness to help the patient improve his or her ability to accept the present reality. Second, it enables the person to handle the negative feelings and emotions that he or she has at a given time. Third, it allows the individual to regulate his or her complex emotions and react in the appropriate ways. Lastly, DBT improves someone's communication skills, which may allow them to strengthen relationships.

Dialectical behavioral therapy operates from the rational process of dialectics, which is based on the idea that everything in this world has opposites and that change happens when one force is stronger than the other. It also works itself out in the form of a thesis, antithesis, and synthesis.[20]

Within dialectics, there are three underlying assumptions: all things are connected, change is continuous and ongoing, and opposites can be interrelated to approach a concept of

---

[19] Psychology Today. (n.d.). Dialectical behavior therapy. Retrieved from https://www.psychologytoday.com/us/therapy-types/dialectical-behavior-therapy

[20] Schimelpfening, N. (2019). Overview of dialectical behavioral therapy. Retrieved from https://www.verywellmind.com/dialectical-behavior-therapy-1067402

a shared truth. In dialectical behavior therapy, after all, the patient and the therapist are working together to solve the problem, as well as the paradox between self-acceptance and personal change to bring about positive changes in someone's life (Schimelpfening, 2019).

Another method that Linehan (1993) used in her DBT book was validation. This means that a therapist can identify with the patient in his or her struggle and tell that his or her actions "make sense" based on the situational context that a person is in.

DBT can be administered in three different settings.

1. Classroom setting where a person is taught how to manage behavior by doing homework and interacting with different people.

2. Individual or one-to-one therapy with a therapist provides the opportunity to share concerns, worries, and ideas with that person.

3. Phone therapy in which a person calls their therapist to receive advice on dealing with challenging and stressful situations.

Four DBT Strategies

People who take DBT sessions are going to use four main strategies, as outlined by Schimelpfening (2019).

Mindfulness

In this strategy, the patient will focus on the here and now and not worry about what's in the past or future. Mindfulness uses extended meditation and concentration therapies that enable a person to achieve balance in life, as well as in how he or she thinks about the world.

Distress Tolerance

Through this technique, the individual learns to accept his or her situation and self. Also, the person is taught to deal with crises and use methods to distract, soothe himself or herself, improve his or her movements, and critically and rationally look at a situation.

Interpersonal Strategies

This strategy allows someone to be assertive in his or her relationships, say, by expressing desires and requirements while also saying "no" to harmful or stressful things. It is about keeping relationships in check and balance.

Regulation of Negative Emotions

Within this method, the patient will learn how to recognize and deal with his or her overwhelming negative emotions. For example, if a person tends to get into emotional tantrums and has difficulty controlling his or her anger, he or she may try counting from one to ten, divert his or her attention to something else, or think of positive thoughts to counter the negative ones. Learning to control emotions is important to develop a positive mindset and deflect negativities.

Conclusion

To sum up, there are several strategies that dialectical behavioral therapy uses to help patients in their day-to-day life, including mindfulness, distress tolerance, interpersonal strategies, and regulation of negative emotions. As a form of cognitive behavior therapy, DBT enables a patient to regulate their thoughts, feelings, and emotions and live a more balanced life by responding to the stressors of daily life in a positive and constructive way.

Chapter 9: Understanding Borderline Personality Disorder (BPD)

Now that you have some understanding of dialectical behavioral therapy, we are going to go into the treatment of borderline personality disorder and how it works. There is a specific program of cognitive behavior therapy that is helpful to those who struggle with this condition, and it is essential to outline all the different aspects of the treatment. Here, we will describe the four modules in each chapter, as well as how the treatment helps patients to achieve their wellness goals. Each chapter gives information about the treatment, strategies for coping with negative emotions, how to live within the moment, and how to accept situations as they are. These are common themes that continue to appear in DBT strategies. The therapist seeks to give the patient information about how to effectively go forward and manage the symptoms of the illness.

What is Borderline Personality Disorder?

Borderline personality disorder (BPD) is a major psychological illness. Its symptoms include unstable moods and emotions, difficulty in handling interpersonal relationships, and erratic behaviors.[21] The condition is found on a list of many personality disorders defined by the

---

[21] Salters-Pedneault, K. (2018). Understanding borderline personality disorder (BPD). Retrieved from https://www.verywellmind.com/what-is-borderline-personality-disorder-bpd-425487

American Psychiatric Association (APA).[22] Such mental health problems usually develop during childhood or adolescence. They continue to progress over a long period; when they are left untreated, the issues can cause severe anxiety and stress. Luckily, there are treatment options available.

Symptoms of BPD

BPD is the root of many problems that practically inhibit a person from enjoying his or her life or achieving goals in work, school or other matters. It can create various relational challenges and negative feelings and behaviors, including:

Negative Self-Image

People who have BPD report having a hard time connecting to their inner selves. They feel severe highs and lows in how they think about themselves. Sometimes these folks feel really good and have a positive self-concept; however, other times, they may feel lousy or down and want to self-harm.

Emotional Insecurity

Patients with borderline personality disorder tend to think like they are on an emotional roller coaster ride because their moods shift quickly. Things may seem chill for a few minutes, but within an hour or two, they become sad and depressed. While moods change suddenly, they can also last for days at a time. Feelings of depression, anxiety, anger,

---

[22] American Psychiatric Association. (n.d.) Diagnostic and Statistical Manual of Mental Disorders (DSM–5). Retrieved from
https://www.psychiatry.org/psychiatrists/practice/dsm

and other emotions can be quite severe for a person.

Risky Behavior

In addition to their emotional and body-image issues, people with BPD also engage in a behavior that can be risky and life-threatening not only to themselves but also to others. This includes alcohol abuse, possession of illegal drugs, and prostitution, among others. They are likely to want to cut themselves as well or, at their worst, commit suicide.

Eating Disorders

BPD patients may develop eating habits that are unhealthy and avoid eating as much as they need to gain nutrients from the foods. If left undiagnosed, the problem can become anorexia or bulimia. This ties into negative body image and or self-concept that a person may have. Its symptoms include (but are not limited to):

1. Feelings of isolation, boredom or emptiness;
2. Challenges with feeling sympathy or empathy for other people;
3. Unhealthy relationships in which a person loves a person for a minute and then hates the other person the next;
4. Feelings of hostility toward others;
5. Strong feelings of anxiety, depression, or other psychiatric conditions;
6. Mood swings that can last from a few minutes to weeks;

7. Unfocused goals and aspirations in one's life; and

8. Fear of being rejected by others.[23]

Causes of BPD

The cause of borderline personality disorder is quite complicated, considering it is not a single thing that it stems from. However, there is a combination of environmental and natural issues that come into play. Here are some factors that might cause BPD to occur in individuals.

Negative and Traumatic Experiences

Many individuals who have received a BPD diagnosis have been victims of child abuse and trauma or witnessed their parents' separation early in life. However, not every patient with the borderline personality disorder has had severe childhood trauma or negative experiences. This is an influencing factor for how a person's psychology may develop.

Brain Chemistry

This one is difficult to grasp because the brain functions in ways that we cannot fully comprehend. Nevertheless, the brain is wired differently in patients with BPD. The diversities are especially marked in an individual's emotional regulation and control of impulses.

Family History

If a mother, father or relative has a borderline personality

---

[23] Cagliostro, D. (2018). Borderline personality disorder: A guide to spotting the signs of borderline personality disorder - BPD. Retrieved from https://www.psycom.net/depression.central.borderline.html

disorder, it increases your risk of developing the same condition. Genetics may play into this.

Getting Treatment for BPD

Living with BPD or being in a relationship with someone who has it can be intensely difficult. Accepting the diagnosis may already pose as a challenge, but getting the treatment is a necessary step in the recovery process. Seeking help, therefore, is an essential aspect of getting better, considering it is the only path towards your health's improvement.

The best way to find help is by contacting the local mental health professional. That may be a counselor, a psychologist or a psychiatrist. Many mental healthcare providers are out there to give you the best, most comprehensive assistance that will get you on the road to recovery for this complex disorder. Because borderline personality disorder requires a long-term care plan, it will take awhile for you to get on track to treating this condition.

Talk therapy will be a form of treatment that must be used to manage the symptoms of the illness. When you talk to a trusted therapist, you will be able to find ways to combat negative emotions, as well as impulsive and self-mutilating behaviors that can harm your body. You have to learn to work with your counselor so that you can receive the long-term treatment and care that you need to see a positive result in the end.

Dealing with Triggers and BPD

Most people with borderline personality disorder have some triggers, which are events or situations that can cause great stress to the patient and can make their symptoms worse.[24] A trigger is a situation, event, or object that causes a person to act out on his or feelings. It can also make the symptoms of BPD worse. The trigger can be something external to a person or something that is internal and happens within a person's mind. There are different things that are common to many people with the illness.

Common Triggers

A relationship is one type of trigger for BPD patients. Some people may have intense feelings of anger or fear that cause them to inflict pain on themselves or even become suicidal following an event that makes them feel criticized, rejected or abandoned (Salters-Pedneault, 2018).

For example, you may feel agitated when you send a message to someone but do not get a timely response. After waiting a few hours, you may think, "He's not calling back. Je must be mad at me." Thoughts race and get out of control, to the extent that you might conclude, "He hates me" or "I have no friends I can trust." With these ideas in mind, intense emotions, anger, and urges to do self-mutilation might arise.

Cognitive Triggers

Cognitive triggers are caused by traumatic events that a person may have had as a child or adolescent. A memory or image can prompt emotional reactions. The memory can be traumatic, but it triggers something that causes a person to

---

[24] Salters-Pedneault, K. (2018). Understanding borderline personality disorder triggers. Retrieved from https://www.verywellmind.com/bpd-triggers-425475

act out on his or her feelings.

Stimuli depend on a variety of factors and differ from one individual to another. An essential aspect of dealing with triggers is knowing what they are and identifying the worst of them all. After having discovered what the trigger is, you can then try to avoid it. For example, you may have nightmares from watching scary movies, which you can avoid by refusing to see them. However, many triggers cannot be prevented, and you have to make an action plan for dealing with them (Salters-Pedneault, 2018). So, you will have to talk to a therapist about what options you can take. The mental health professional will be able to help you manage your emotions and deal with the triggers.

Managing Triggers

Learning to handle the BPD stimuli is one of the critical steps to getting better and improving your psychological state. If you know what can easily set you off, you can learn how to effectively deal with your emotional responses healthily and constructively. Living with your triggers enables you to live with empowerment over your reactions to circumstances because you know how you normally act out on your feelings and stop yourself from going off and doing something that you might regret later. It gives you a sense of self-control that you can demonstrate before others. Let's give a practical example of someone who had a trigger and used it to avoid a confrontation.

Case Study

Thomas was often disturbed by the shouts and raised voices of the people around him because he could recall a time when he was a child and his father would yell at him constantly for not doing everything the right way. The father was deeply critical of his son and would berate him even in front of others. Thomas had a childhood trauma from this beratement that he received; thus, whenever he heard loud shouting, he would feel anxious and have a panic attack. Gradually, over time, Thomas was able to recover from this, and he no longer thought that people were yelling at him whenever someone would raise their voice. Thomas learned how to practice mindfulness and react positively to whenever his feelings got triggered. He no longer felt the intense fear and negative feelings of anxiety that came when hearing shouts. Thomas, who is now 31 years old, knows he has this trigger and uses it as a way to live with his condition and diagnosis of BPD.

Conclusion

To sum up, the borderline personality disorder is a complex condition that requires intensive treatment and intervention from a specialist. It is an illness that enables a patient to recognize his or her triggers, what causes his or her stress or anxiety, and develop ways to be proactive in treating such a condition. While medication may be required, it is possible to try dialectical behavior therapy, which is a proven CBT method that will help the patient to proactively deal with BPD and manage the symptoms of intense and overwhelming emotions that can easily hinder and cause pain to a patient.

Chapter 10: Practicing Positive Mindfulness

As we mentioned above, there are four modules that you follow in dialectical behavioral therapy. They can be used to treat borderline personality disorder. In the following, we will look at more depth at the DBT treatment modules for borderline personality disorder, along with examples to guide each one of the modules. We hope that you will find it to be helpful in your continued exploration of dialectical behavioral therapy. We will show what you can do to deal with your complex emotions with the different DBT strategies that are taught by therapists. The first is practicing mindfulness.

Mindfulness

Mindfulness provides a foundation for DBT. It is based on Eastern Zen Buddhism and also includes Western contemplative practices.[25] Mindfulness enables a person to be aware of their thoughts, feelings, and behaviors. Through this practice, an individual can take responsibility for his or her life in a different way (Arnold, 2008). After all, mindfulness has been proven to be able to help a person regulate his or her emotions and work on accepting feelings and making changes in his or her life.

When doing dialectical behavior therapy, a person will practice mindfulness and be concerned with three different states of mind: wise mind, logical mind, and emotional

---

[25] Arnold, T. (2008). Core mindfulness: Dialectical behavior therapy (DBT). Retrieved from https://www.goodtherapy.org/blog/dialectical-behavior-therapy-dbt-core-mindfulness/

mind. The first is the ideal state that a person may want to reach in this lifetime. The other two comprise what a person strives for with a wise mind. The logical mind, to be specific, is used when someone does math problems, looks at a map, or performs other rational tasks.

The logical mind deals with empirical facts and concrete tasks that a person can accomplish. The last state of mind is the emotional state, which allows a person to experience the most profound feelings and act out of emotional reaction to a situation. The latter is usually connected to impulsive decisions and is also known as the "hot" state of mind because of the intensity of reaction that someone gives during a heated moment.

In the wise mind, a person is grounded and is aware of emotions and knows how to react to the various circumstances. Even when prompted negatively, he or she can recognize the feelings of anger or frustration and respond appropriately to anyone.

It is essential that the individual learns to be aware of his or feelings. The skills that BPD patients acquire from DBT sessions include observation, description, and participation.[26] Let's look at a more detailed description of these skills.

Observation

The first ability to acquire in mindfulness is observation. In this part, the individual should become aware of thoughts, emotions, situations, and behaviors without changing

---

[26] Grohol, J. M. (2018). An overview of dialectical behavior therapy. Retrieved from https://psychcentral.com/lib/an-overview-of-dialectical-behavior-therapy/

them. Instead of trying to modify or respond to it, the person directly collects data from experience. This skill includes note-taking to record what is happening around him or her.

Description

After having observed a person's situation, he or she can then describe an occurrence. With more description of the event, an individual can have more empathy and exercise self-control. During this phase, he or she analyzes the situation with the data collected and separates fact from perception.

Participation

With the third skill, the person participates in the current moment and becomes more aware of the present and lives in every moment constructively.

Other skills in which you may use mindfulness include how you judge the world. For example, taking a non-evaluative approach to a tensed situation makes it better and more uplifting for someone. Rather than seeing a situation as good or bad, he or she can holistically look at a circumstance and understand how to deal with it.

Also, a person who practices mindfulness can live in the moment and focus on one task at a time while not worrying about how a situation will turn out. Instead of thinking about many things at once, the individual can do mono-tasking, which is more effective and productive as a means to improve one's state of mind. It also enables a person to achieve his or her goals.

It is crucial to develop skills in mindfulness that will help you in your DBT program. Formal mindfulness helps you focus your attention and improve awareness of situations. For example, you may hold your breath to observe your breathing pattern, as well as what's going on in your body during that time. How fast or slow is your breathing, for one? Similarly, you can go on a long walk into the woods to become aware of your senses. You might also pay attention to the sights and sounds of things that are around you, including the noise that leaves make when crunched under your feet, the rain that is gently dropping on the roof or the chirping of the birds nearby.

Mindfulness can be practiced anytime and anywhere. You do not have to be in a therapy room or with a therapist to practice it. You might be sitting in a meeting and trying to focus, but you are worried about something that has captured your attention. Mindfulness allows you to drown out these distractions and bring your concentration back to the activity that you are doing. It is about noticing the disturbances that you experience and bringing you back to the task at hand. The patients who are doing dialectical behavior therapy should realize that they need to familiarize themselves with such distractions. Nevertheless, they also should know that it is impossible to get rid of all the disturbances; that's why they must learn how to cope with these sources of discomfort and stress.

Tips on Practicing Mindfulness

1. Start thinking about one task at a time. Do not try to do too much at once. You need to be mindful of each task that you are doing to lessen errors and repeating the activity.

2. Practice making observations out loud. If you are looking at things outside, you can be mindful by noticing them and then voicing out your thoughts. It helps you to do a meditative practice of externalizing your ideas.

3. Take note of your distractions. You should notice when your mind starts to drift in a given situation. Be aware of the situation but try not to react to it.

4. Be gentle with yourself. While you begin to practice mindfulness, you need to take care of yourself since it will take some time to develop the technique and have a more peaceful state of being and thinking.

Techniques and Exercises for Using Mindfulness in Your Life

There are several techniques and exercises that you can do to begin your journey towards mindfulness today.[27] These methods can provide you with ways to relax and de-stress after long days and enable you to feel better about different aspects of your life.

Meditation

This seems like a stereotypical thing to do, but it is useful in getting you to relax and enjoy the present moment. So, take a minute to sit on the floor and close your eyes. Light a

---

[27] Positive Psychology Program: Your One-Stop Positive Psychology Resource. (2017). 22 mindfulness exercises, techniques, and activities for adults (+PDFs). Retrieved from https://positivepsychologyprogram.com/mindfulness-exercises-techniques-activities

candle and play some low-key music that will engage your ears and allow you to de-stress and unplug from your busy life. You can think about different things that will enable you to get your mind off of the stressful circumstances that you are going through.

Guided Meditation Through Audio Recordings

In this kind of meditation, you are guided through various thoughts in your mind. The recording indicates what you should think about as you are meditating, and usually there is music that accompanies the recording. This technique can also be done in a dim room that does not have a lot of noise. You can use some noise-canceling headphones to block out all the background sounds if you wish.

Do the Raisin Exercise

This exercise involves looking at any food, but we can use the example of a raisin. The participant looks at the fruit and describes how it looks, feels, how their skin responds to moving it, as well as the smell and taste of the object. As the person looks at it, he or she can focus on the here and now and not on anything else.

The Body Scan

In this practice, the individual is going to concentrate on each part of his or her body. It is as if he or she is doing a body scan. The participants lie on their backs and sit still during the exercise. In the beginning, people focus on how they are breathing, including the rhythm of inhaling and exhaling. Then, the guru shows the participants how to pay attention to the body until they become aware of all the parts and how they feel. The body scan runs from the head to the neck to the chest and down to the toes and feet. After the learners are done, they can open his eyes and feel very relaxed.

Mindful Observation

In this exercise, you look out a window and observe everything that you see outside. Instead of naming things, such as bird, person or tree, though, you should notice the colors, pictures, and other figures that are out there. You should pay close attention to leaves blowing, the grass swaying in a breeze, and the different shapes of the structures. Try to remain focused on the task at hand, but do not get too distracted by any of them. If you need to take a break, you can get away from the window for a few minutes.

Mindful Listening

Such an exercise is a form of therapy that you can do with other people. You think of one thing that you are stressed or worried about, as well as another thing that you look forward to in the future, and then share it with other participants. The therapist will ask everyone to think about how they are talking about their thoughts. You should observe your thinking patterns and emotions as you speaking and listen to others. Then, you should all reflect on the practice together.

Self-Compassion Break

Self-compassion is a way to cope with life's difficulties by showing kindness to yourself whenever you are feeling stressed or overwhelmed. When burdened by different situations, you can take a break out of your busy schedule, close your eyes, breathe in and out or give yourself a hug or another kind of embrace. Utter some supportive phrases as well, such as, "I know this is hard, but you are doing a good job keeping yourself together. You are awesome!" You have to practice self-affirming language since it will help you get through any hurdle at a given time.

Hold-and-Stretch Exercise

In this exercise, you tense up your muscles and focus on the parts of your body that are causing you to feel stressed or uptight. You gently put pressure on the muscle and concentrate on each part of the body. Then, you release the stress and tension after a few seconds.

Five-Senses Exercise

Through this technique, you look at five different things that you can see, hear, feel, touch, and taste to notice how they appear to you. It is a quick exercise that can bring you to a state of mindfulness in a pinch if you feel down. The five senses can enable you to become aware of your present state within a short period.

Three-Minute Breathing Technique

In this exercise, you spend three minutes looking at how you breathe. During the first minute, you ask yourself, "How am I doing at this moment?" Think about what you are feeling, thinking, and sensing within that period. The second minute should be spent thinking about your breathing pattern. In the last minute, you should focus exclusively on breathing and how it affects the whole body.

Practice Mindful Eating

This method involves concentrating on what you eat. Before putting the food in your mouth, hold and feel it in your hands. Notice the different aspects of it, including its texture, smell, taste, et cetera. Try to eat slowly to be able to do so.

Think About Your Thinking

This exercise requires you to think about your breathing and your body, as well as your thoughts. You should be aware of what ideas are coming to your head and judge them one at a time. If your mind wanders or strays from the task, you can gently guide your mind back to the meditation phase.

Mindfulness Technique for Anger Management

Mindfulness can put your mind at ease when you feel like exploding in anger. With this technique, you can calm your emotions and think clearly (Cullen et al, 2016). First, you should sit in a comfortable position or chair. Make sure that your feet are touching the floor or any flat surface underneath. You should practice deep breathing to be able to fill your lungs with air well, too. Think about a time when you recently got angry, when you were able to cope with a difficult situation. Think about the strong feeling that you experienced at that moment, as well as how your body reacted to this anger.

Notice how different parts of your body are tensed or stressed and observe what is happening. Then, be compassionate to yourself. You may say, "It is natural to be angry. It's okay. This, too, will pass." Then, get rid of your anger by uttering a simple "goodbye." Once you manage to concentrate on your breathing again, you can calm down. This technique should be repeated as many times as you need to. It should also be worked up gradually from milder episodes of anger to more severe and explosive ones.

Stare at a Circle and Reflect on It for a Minute or Two

This exercise allows you to slow down and focus on one thing at a time so that you can concentrate on the circle. Think about your thoughts, reflect on what you are thinking about, and assess its validity and plausibility.

Case Study

Timothy (18) was recently diagnosed with borderline personality disorder. He somewhat had attention-deficit hyperactivity disorder (ADHD) as well. Many times, he would get upset and angry because he was slower than the other students and become distracted easily by his work. Timothy would go into some emotional tantrums at school, too. He would get frustrated at one point and blow up in the middle of class. Often, his teacher would send him out of the classroom because he could not control himself. Later, Timothy's parents took him to a psychiatrist to find out how to treat his condition. The doctor recommended dialectical behavioral therapy to him.

The first thing that the therapist taught Timothy was to practice mindfulness. He learned a variety of exercises. In one exercise, Timothy would stretch his muscles, pause at his desk, close his eyes, and count to ten. He would also focus on his breathing. This way, Timothy could take a time-out whenever he needed to collect his thoughts. As the teenager learned how to do deep breathing and take a pause when he was getting upset, he understood how to successfully manage his symptoms by going to regular therapy sessions with his therapist. Also, Timothy attended group therapy sessions with other young adults who had developed the same disorder. It helped him tremendously in staying on the path to recovery. Amazingly, within one year of being in the program, Timothy got the symptoms of both BPD and ADHD under control.

Conclusion

As you can see, mindfulness is a powerful tool for managing life even for someone with a mental health condition. All of the techniques mentioned earlier are proven to help the person to be in touch with how he or she is feeling about everyday situations and permits him or her to pause and concentrate on one thing at a time. Among the key issues that it examines is how an individual breathes, as well as how his or her body reacts to the stress, anger, or other feelings that he or she is experiencing. By pausing and taking time to reflect, he or she can examine his or her thought processes and practice self-compassion to calm down. These techniques can be exercised by meditating at home or anywhere that a person may be. You can even practice a few of them when you are at work or doing some activity.

Chapter 11: Learning How to Regulate Emotions

The second module that is used in dialectical behavioral therapy is emotion regulation, which helps a person understand how his emotions work, what urges go with every emotion, and whether to react to or ignore these urges. It also aids in reducing an individual's vulnerability, increasing reaction to negative and unwanted feelings, and improving mental health.[28] In this chapter, we will talk about how emotions work and how DBT enables a person to manage his or her feelings.

Why Do We Use Emotion Regulation?

We use emotional regulation because it allows a person to deal proactively with his or her emotions and raise emotional resiliency whenever the negative feelings come up, according to an article from Sunrise Residential Treatment Center (2017). It helps someone cope with the painful emotions that he or she may have at the moment. Furthermore, the strategies allow an individual to prevent disastrous scenarios from occurring.

What are Emotions?

Every emotion that we have is a response to a given situation, and it always has a purpose. Often, we have a certain "gut instinct" about a person that we get in touch with, a.k.a. a stomach-clenching experience. When you

---

[28] Sunrise Residential Treatment Center. (2017). What are DBT emotion regulation skills? Retrieved from https://www.sunrisertc.com/dbt-emotion-regulation-skills/

meet someone you don't know, you may think that they are a good person, but your intuition tells you that something is a little off about them. This kind of reaction is based on the emotions that you have. However, it is vital to note that feelings are not always accurate and do not correspond with reality every time. Nevertheless, you should listen to them and what they have to tell you to avoid finding yourself in a messy situation.

Emotions are powerful things. For people who are "feelers," they tend to have an over-reliance on feelings to guide their decisions. Many individuals with mental illnesses have heightened awareness of their emotions and are more reactive to the things that affect how they feel. Because of that, it is essential that we find ways to treat the condition by focusing on how a person is feeling at a given time.

Emotions can be influenced by those around us. When a person experiences pain due to a broken relationship, a trusted friend can help encourage him or her to move forward. However, if people gossip about that individual, others may start to feel negatively toward him or her.

There is a particular case that is called "fight or flight" in which a person immediately reacts to a situation based on their emotional experience. They do not have any time to think about it at once; their response depends on how they are feeling at the moment. It is a type of instinctual response that a body may have, for example, when the individual senses a dangerous situation. Every time an emotion comes up, therefore, he or she should observe how he or she is feeling and not judge what it is before doing an observation. One critical first step in emotional regulation is identifying how you are feeling and thinking about what this emotion is revealing to you about the truth of a situation. You have to validate whether or not a given feeling is real based on empirical evidence to support the case.

As humans, we will never be able to control our feelings and reactions to them completely. However, we can influence them in different ways. The skills that a person develops through the practice will enable him or her to manage the particularly difficult and overpowering emotions of anger and anxiety, among others.

About Emotional Regulation

One of the most important aspects of emotional regulation is enabling an individual to recognize negative and painful emotions in a morally neutral way. Patients must see that they experience feelings and that it is entirely normal to deal with powerful ones at a time. Despite that, they should not carry moral judgments on the unusually strong emotions that they have. Rather than avoiding these emotions, the patients of dialectical behavioral therapy learn how to monitor and deal with their complex emotions.

What is Emotional Dysregulation?

Emotional regulation is a process used to control an individual's emotional response to given situations. Emotional dysregulation is the opposite of that, in which a person is unable to control his or her feelings.[29]

In emotional dysregulation, a person is motivated to act

---

[29] Positive Psychology Program: Your One-Stop Positive Psychology Resource. (2018). Emotion regulation worksheets & strategies: Improve your DBT skills. Retrieved from https://positivepsychologyprogram.com/emotion-regulation-worksheets-strategies-dbt-skills/

based on an internal or external event that evokes an intense feeling. The cognitive response to the emotion leads to an increase in heart rate and other physiological experiences related to stress and anxiety. Following these feelings, the behavior that comes after is potentially explosive or harmful.

Individuals who have emotional dysregulation tend to overreact to situations of minor importance or gravity. They might scream, cry or blame others around them. They are very sensitive to their environment, as well as deal with unstable moods and emotions.

Strategies and Techniques to Use in Regulating Emotions

Dialectical behavioral therapy focuses on practical skills that enable an individual to solve problems in his or her life. Your therapist will help you develop strategies for managing emotions. Here are some techniques that you may anticipate.

1. Labeling the Emotion

One of the best ways to regulate emotions is labeling what you are feeling. DBT encourages the patient to use detailed labels to identify his or her emotions. Therapists say that you have to know exactly what you feel; the more detailed you become, the better. DBT patients discover the difference between various emotions, including the primary and secondary ones.

Primary emotions are the body's reaction to an event or trigger that a person might experience, while the secondary feelings are the response to the primary emotions. Feelings are natural responses to given circumstances, including the death of a loved one or being angry when someone is rude to you. On the other hand, secondary emotions are the ones that an individual can control without getting into an emotional frenzy. They can be potentially dangerous and destructive, though, as they cause us to act out negatively on feelings.

The key part of DBT is recognizing the morally neutral aspects of emotions and rejecting the assumption that there is a right or wrong way to feel at any given time. The appropriate DBT response to things is to say, "It's okay to feel angry. It's a natural way to feel." With dialectical behavioral therapy, you have to recognize emotions as real and needing a reaction, but you should not try to ignore what it is.

2. Learning to Let Go

Letting go is a difficult skill to master because someone can be completely wrapped up in how he or she is feeling about a situation. As humans, we tend to get stuck when we try to pull ourselves out of negative emotional cycles. Rather than letting go, we end up holding onto the situations, as if clutching them with a death-grip on a steering wheel. When we accept the suffering from our emotions, though, we can face them with more resolve and confidence than before. Then, we look at the situation with more courage because we know that we can stand up to the monster that is better known as emotional negativity and deal with it. Here are some steps that you can follow to let go:

    a. Just observe what you feel without judging it. Watch how it will unfold.

b. Try to say to yourself: "This is just an emotion that I am feeling. I will not feel this way tomorrow."

c. Embrace your emotions. Instead of rejecting or fighting our feelings, we should welcome them as a part of our humanity.

3. Taking Care of Yourself

A healthy mind starts with having a healthy body, and you can have both by eating nutritious meals, getting your daily exercise, sleeping well at night, and avoiding drugs or excessive alcohol use. Physical feelings of fatigue, sickness or hunger can negatively influence emotions. For example, you might hear someone say that they are "hangry." The spelling is not wrong since the term means that you are angry as a result of the hunger that you are presently experiencing. Anyone usually does not make the best decisions when physically exhausted or hungry.

4. Focusing on Positivity

Another strategy is to remain positive at all times. You should enjoy the nice emotions that you experience and thrive in them. Allow yourself to smile and be happy when you experience a good time at a party, an evening at home, or other moments.

5. Allowing Yourself to Have Fun

Life is too short to make it all about work. You should try to enjoy every once in a while. Say, go to a movie. Treat yourself to dinner at a new restaurant. Hang out with your friends. Make an effort to enjoy life. The more you do so, the more positive emotions you will have, and the happier and more fulfilled you will feel.

6. Repairing Broken Relationships

To fix the challenges in your relationships, you should attempt to make reconciliation. Try to strengthen ties with people you are having trouble relating to or rekindle lost friendships. It is important for you to maintain current relationships or create new ones to boost your emotional stability.

7. Living With Fewer Worries

To avoid being caught up in negative emotion, you should try to avert your worries to positive things so that you won't become anxious and worried about things in your life. There is a lot to worry about these days, but you can take a break from all of them and concentrate on things that will be positive and uplifting. It makes a big difference in your overall morale.

8. Noticing Your Arousal Pattern

When you start to feel aroused emotionally by any given situation, take note of it and write down the details about it in a journal or on a piece of paper. This way, you can remember when it happens again and reflect on how you can respond to it next time.

9. Hitting Your "Pause" Button

One of the best things you can do for yourself when you are tempted to act out on negative emotions is to hit your "pause" button. Stop! Hold the thought. Count from one to ten. Observe what is going on around you and in your mind. Then, think about the big picture. Take a deep breath before responding to the event. The "pause" button enables a person to have a broader perspective on how they are feeling and lets him or her to stay still and reflect before reacting to a situation.

10. Distinguishing Healthy and Unhealthy Ways to Regulate Emotions

You should also think about how you can cope with your feelings. There are always healthy and unhealthy ways to go about this. Here are some examples of positive and healthy ways to regulate emotions:

- Meditation
- Talk therapy with friends
- Getting enough sleep
- Self-monitoring with negative thoughts
- Noticing when you need to take a break
- Writing out your thoughts
- Exercising regularly

Here are a few unhealthy ways to deal with your emotions:

- Using social media too much and posting a lot on Facebook to vent about your feelings or monitoring others' activities.
- Social withdrawal
- Self-mutilative acts
- Abuse of alcohol or illegal substances

These activities may initially seem helpful and make you

feel good, but they can lead to damage to your health and well-being in the long-term. Instead of resorting to such options, you should try to do things that are both positive and fulfilling to be able to uplift your emotions.

Case Study

Irene is a mathematics teacher at Johnson High School in Virginia. She struggled with self-acceptance before becoming a teacher. Over time, she developed an intensely perfectionistic tendency to self-flagellate whenever she made a mistake. For example, during her first semester as a teacher at Johnson High School, Irene ended up copying the data for her grades from her grade book to the software online and lost most of it. She beat herself up because of this matter and started to cut herself with a knife. She smoked a whole pack of cigarettes before proceeding to burn herself with the remnants of the stick. Her husband saw that she was doing this and said, "Irene, what are you doing? We need to see a therapist today."

Irene realized that she needed help and that she had been struggling to deal with her anxiety and accept her flaws and mistakes. So, Irene agreed to go to her therapist, who was able to help her make sense of what was causing her difficulties. The mental health professional taught her how to practice mindfulness and focus on the present. The therapist told her, "Irene, you have to concentrate on the here and now. Do not dwell on your mistakes or keep them running through your mind all the time. I think that you have the tendency to overthink things, and that is not the best idea. Instead, you have to go with the flow and only meditate and focus on what is right in front of you. There's nothing you can do about the past. You only need to think about the present and how you can change your future." She even added, "You need to replace all that negativity that is in your mind with positive and encouraging thoughts." It was crucial for Irene to realize that she needed to push out all the negative ideas that she had about herself and accept and move past her errors while committing not to do it again. After four modules of training, Irene was able to overcome her self-mutilating tendencies and negative self-talk. She was able to manage her emotions effectively as well.

You can now see that from this case study that someone was able to overcome negative self-talk and self-mutilation, which are two familiar activities to those individuals with borderline personality disorder. In the following chapter, we will show in depth all the ways that a person can be treated for this disorder with the DBT process.

Conclusion

To conclude, our emotions are an essential part of who we are. Every human emotion has a purpose in our lives. We should not ignore them; instead, we need to learn how to deal with them. The first step in the process of managing emotions is identifying and observing a particular feeling. Then, we can decide how to act on those emotions whether constructively or destructively. However, that may not always work because we tend to react to situations without consciously thinking or reflecting from our fight-or-flight instinct. By training ourselves to respond in a positive and uplifting way, we can recognize the validity of our emotions and react in ways that will help us to act with maturity and wisdom. This can take a while to master completely, but it is helpful to anyone who is trying to manage their emotions, as well as the symptoms of borderline personality disorder.

Chapter 12: Developing Interpersonal Effectiveness

The third module in dialectical behavioral therapy is interpersonal effectiveness. It is an important skill to have because the quality of our relationships depends on how well we communicate with others. DBT patients are taught how to approach conversations in ways that will be thoughtful, considerate toward others, and intentional. Individuals are also trained when it comes to managing with stress and intense emotions and avoiding overreacting to them while communicating with others. Marsha Linehan (1993), the founder of DBT, identified three kinds of effectiveness that need to be considered when dealing with interpersonal relationships.

1. Objective effectiveness
2. Relationship effectiveness
3. Self-respect effectiveness

For all situations, these factors should be examined and prioritized. Let's look at the meaning of each one of these effectiveness priorities.

Objective effectiveness considers a goal or purpose for an interaction that has an achievable outcome. Suzette Bray (2013) explains how there are acronyms to go with each of these effectiveness priorities.

DBT uses the acronym DEAR MAN for objective

effectiveness. [30]

D - Describe a situation with precise details and without judging the circumstances.

E - Express your feelings to the other person.

A - Assert what you want or not want from a situation.

R - Reinforce the reason why you want an outcome to happen and reward the person who positively responds to your request.

M - Mindful practice is important in any given moment while concentrating on the goal.

A - Appear calm, relaxed, and confident.

N - Negotiate with others to get what you want and settle any kinds of issues.

For relationship effectiveness, the DBT acronym is called GIVE.

G - Gentle approach to the other person entails coming to someone in a loving, non-threatening way.

I - Interested act when listening to them to another person is key.

V - Validate someone else's feelings, wishes, and opinions. Let the other person know that you have acknowledged them.

E - Easy and relaxed attitude toward others can be shown

---

[30] Bray, S. (2013). Interpersonal effectiveness in dialectical behavioral therapy. Retrieved from https://www.goodtherapy.org/blog/interpersonal-effectiveness-dialectical-behavior-therapy-dbt-0416134

by smiling and using humor to help soften the mood.

These acronyms simplify the development of interpersonal skills. They help a person figure out how to deal with people while transparently communicating their needs and intentions and without making the other person "read their mind." This system enables someone to talk to anyone in a straightforward yet respectful manner.

Goals of Interpersonal Skills in DBT

Interpersonal skills are crucial when it comes to developing a harmonious life with everyone you meet. Thus, it is vital for you to learn how to relate to others in meaningful ways. Instead of being rude or demanding, to be specific, you should try more kind and softer tactics to get what you want. By making demands with kindness, you can increase your chances of having the other party react positively to the request and do what you ask them to do. It is a way of negotiating with another person.

When people are making negotiations, Spradlin (2003) suggested to ask oneself different questions regarding various aspects of the relationship.[31]

Priorities:

- Are my goals important?
- Is this relationship delicate or broken in any way?
- Will I risk my self-respect by doing this or that?

---

[31] Spradlin, S.E. (2003). *Don't let your emotions run your life: How dialectical behavior therapy can put you in control.* Oakland, CA: New Harbinger Publications, Inc.

Capability:

- Can this person give me what I want?
- Do I have what the person wants from me?

Timing:

- Can this person listen to me right now?
- Is there a good time for me to make my request?
- Is this a wrong time?

Homework:

- Do I know enough about this person who I am talking to?
- Do I have everything I need to know about this request?

You can see that it is essential to have excellent communication skills to be able to live a balanced and meaningful life. Yet, not everyone can communicate well. There is always room for growth and development in this area. Research has shown that improving interpersonal skills leads to positive results for patients who have a borderline personality disorder.

Activities That Might Improve Your Interpersonal Skills

The best way to improve your interpersonal skill is by practicing your interactions with others. Here are some activities that you can do with a group to practice how to communicate with others.[32] You can also do some roleplaying and dialoguing to help simulate real-life situations.

1. Try Not to Listen

In this activity, a group of people gets broken into pairs. For each pair, one person speaks first as the other person listens. Partner A is allowed to talk about any topic of his or her interest for two minutes. Partner B makes it clear that he or she is not listening to any word that Partner A is saying. Instead of saying anything, they communicate with body language how they are feeling about it. Partner B then does the same with Partner A. The group will find that it is tough to continue talking when their partner does not want to listen. You can see the power of using body language and how that affects a person's overall attitude.

After the members of the group are finished with the game, they can have a feedback session in which they talk about what happened. They can log the feelings that they had, such as:

- I felt angry and resentful.
- I felt that he or she did not appreciate what I was talking about.
- I could not continue talking.
- I felt that I was very undervalued in this

---

[32] Positive Psychology Program: Your One-Stop Positive Psychology Resource. (2019). Interpersonal effectiveness: 9 worksheets & examples. Retrieved from https://positivepsychologyprogram.com/interpersonal-effectiveness/

conversation.

- He or she frustrated me.

Next, group members need to take note of the behaviors that their partner was showing, which gave away the fact that they were not listening, including:

- Avoiding eye contact
- Yawning or stretching
- Looking away from the person
- Keeping a blank or bored expression on the face
- Looking at one's phone or other things

Although this exercise is an exaggeration of what it looks like when a person is not listening to you, it can help you see how you should behave in a given social situation and know what things to avoid.

Case Study Example

Jim and Johnson were in a coffee shop while having a conversation. They practice what it looks like to not listen to each other. First, Jim talked about his promotion at the new job, and Johnson fidgeted and looked away, yawned, or stayed on his phone nearly the whole time.

Jim: Johnson, I have some exciting news to tell you! I got a promotion at my office! I'm so excited. Let me tell you about what happened.

Johnson: Wow, congratulations! That's great news.

Jim: First, my boss came in and congratulated me. Then,

he led me into his office where he told me about all the accomplishments and contributions, I have made to the company recently. He was so happy.

Johnson: Oh, really? (Looking away and yawning and then looking down at his phone). Wait a second.

Jim: Okay, no problem. I'll keep talking.

Johnson: (still on his phone)

Jim: Are you going to look away from your phone? Please listen to me!!! Johnson!

Johnson: Sorry, I had an important text to attend to.

In this situation, Johnson was demonstrating an inattentive and rude behavior by not listening to Jim. Evidently, Jim is excited about his promotion and wants the attention of his friend without any evidence of interest. Hence, the situation is quite frustrating for him. Jim feels devalued and underappreciated. Later, after this episode, the two talk again about what happened, and Johnson offers an apology to Jim.

The two talk.

Jim: Johnson, I wanted to talk to you and tell you how I really feel. You really hurt my feelings. I wanted you to listen to me when I told you about the new development in my career. It would have been nice if you had paid attention or at least asked me a question or two about the promotion.

Johnson: I recognize that I was rude, and I'm sorry I did that to you, Jim. It was my fault, bro. I didn't mean to do that. I just got distracted. It happens sometimes. I will try to focus next time.

Jim: Thanks. I appreciate that. I forgive you.

2. Sabotage Game

This game should be conducted with at least two to three groups of four to five people. In each group, tell the members to take ten minutes to brainstorm and think of all the ways that they can sabotage a project. The ideas they come up with can be anything. They merely need to think of something that will disrupt the flow of the work and frustrate everyone. Once the groups have provided a list of things that can drive them up the wall, you can gather everyone together and have a feedback session. Then, the instructor writes them on a whiteboard in front of the room, form new groups, and have each group talk about what makes a successful group project.

3. Count the Squares

In this game, you can encourage groups to interact meaningfully and passionately. All you need to do is display an image with different squares within the image and then have group members count the number of squares in the picture. You can do this process in small groups or even pairs. It can be a good process of encouraging detailed collaboration.

4. Non-Verbal Introductions

In this fun exercise, one person introduces himself to one other person in a group and talks about different interesting things about each other. Once every pair has talked together and discovered new things about one another, then the focus shifts back to the group. For the next step, each person must introduce his or her partner to the rest of the group but cannot use words or props. Instead, they must introduce the other using actions. It is a great way to help people understand how to communicate using verbal and nonverbal cues.

Effective Communication

The way to improve communication with others is through listening and reading their cues and expressions. This is something that you should be able to pick up on the more you hang out with people. If you remain concentrated on speaking directly to someone, then you will find that you can communicate with them. This does not require you to be an expert communicator at all; it's just basic conversational skills. You should demonstrate an interest in others and what they have to say to achieve that. Many people are passionate about one or two topics that they're interested in and will be willing to open up and share with you what's on their heart and mind. You should see that this level of vulnerability does not come automatically and that you are not entitled to receive it either. It is something that someone will do only if they trust you and believe that you will listen to them. Therefore, it is crucial that you show an interest in others' thoughts. Too much of our society demonstrates a lack of care in that department. People are so selfish these days, to the extent that they cannot be bothered about what others think. This level of selfishness has caused a lot of strife and discord among various people.

Conclusion

Learning how to communicate is one of the most powerful tools that a person can use to get over the hindrances in life and emotional challenges. Many people with borderline personality disorder do not know how to relate well with others; that's why they sign up for dialectical behavioral therapy.

DBT provides patients with group counseling sessions that allow everyone to talk with each other regarding various issues. Together, they solve problems and do meaningful role plays and games that help them simulate real-life situations and act out how they should behave. It allows participants to rehearse their reactions in social situations as well. These DBT strategies teach individuals about the importance of collaboration and developing rapport and harmony between group members to accomplish goals and objectives within a program. Group therapy is something that should be recommended to individuals who are seeking to improve their interpersonal communication skills and have more harmonious and supportive relationships. It's something that you have to work on throughout your life, but it is especially helpful for people who need to have their mental health conditions treated. Therefore, we recommend that you look into DBT and group therapy as possible treatment options in developing positive relationships with your peers, colleagues, and superiors.

Chapter 13: Practicing Distress Tolerance

The final module that is used in dialectical behavioral therapy involves practicing distress tolerance. This is a skill that is used to deal with the overwhelming and intolerable emotions that can cause high levels of stress and anxiety in a person. In this module, the patient will learn how to manage pain and distress as they come to him or her. Many traditional approaches teach that it is best to avoid stressful situations, but with this technique, the patient can understand why and how he or she should confront the challenges head-on and face his or her fears and anxieties.

One key aspect of distress tolerance is the ability to radically accept a situation. That means the person accepts that there are things about reality that he or she cannot change. When someone admits that he or she does not have control over everything, the buildup of negative feelings that can spiral out of whack may reduce significantly. Within the distress tolerance module of DBT, there are different skills that a person can acquire to deal with challenging situations. [33]

Creating Distractions

The first skill enables a patient to distract himself or herself from an anxiety-inducing situation by focusing on more pleasant thoughts or activities. This is taught through the ACCEPTS acronym.

---

[33] Bray, S. (2013). Distress tolerance in dialectical behavior therapy. Retrieved from https://www.goodtherapy.org/blog/distress-tolerance-dialectical-behavior-therapy-0117134

A is for **Activity**. The patient engages in activities and gets sidetracked with healthy habits, hobbies, and exercise.

C is for **Contributing**. The patient contributes to the needs of others and offers his or her help in a thoughtful and caring manner.

C is for **Comparing**. The patient compares himself or herself to less fortunate individuals and feels grateful for what he or she has.

E is for **Emotion**. The person identifies the current negative emotion and acts in a way that is contrary to the feeling, such as singing or dancing when experiencing sadness or depression.

P is for **Pushing Away**. The person leaves the current situation and focuses on something that is more positive or uplifting.

T is for **Thoughts**. In this situation, the person diverts his or her attention from the negative thoughts and does distracting activities like solving a word puzzle.

S is for **Sensations**. The person distracts himself or herself by making the other senses work. E.g., holding a cup of hot water or enjoying a warm foot bath.

Self-Soothing

The second skill is called self-soothing. In this technique, the patients will use the five senses to help them receive solace and peace within themselves.

Vision

The individual can look outside and visit a park and look

around at the birds, trees, flowers, landscape, and other natural surroundings.

Hearing

The patient listens to music or enjoys the sound of nature. He or she may also listen to the sound of the waves at the sea or enjoy listening to the voice of a friend or relative.

Smell

The person uses his or her favorite fragrance and sprays it to experience a relaxing sensation. Also, scented candles can be used.

Taste

The individual enjoys a delicious meal with some friends.

Touch

The person may touch animals or hug someone. Any kind of physical contact can help someone in the midst of self-soothing.

Improving the Moment

The third skill a person can use in DBT is improving the moment. For this one, the patient should remember the acronym IMPROVE.

I is for **Imagery**. The person imagines a relaxing place or environment. He or she may also imagine the negative feelings going away.

M is for **Meaning**. The patient makes meaning out of the experience of pain or difficulty in a given situation.

P is for **Prayer**. The patient prays to God or a higher being for strength to overcome the present issues.

R is for **Relaxation**. The patient can practice deep breathing and relax his or her muscles. He or she can also listen to music, watch a comedy movie, drink a warm drink or enjoy a hot shower.

O is for **One Thing at a Time**. The individual strives to focus on only one thing at a time and not think about anything else.

V is for **Vacation**. For this, the patient takes a temporary break from a challenging situation by taking a day off from work, going on a trip, fasting from technology or merely calling for a timeout.

E is for **Encouragement**. The patient practices positive self-talk to help himself or herself cope with stressful incidents.

Focusing on Cue-Controlled Relaxation

The fourth technique to use is called cue-controlled relaxation.

This method is useful if you want to reduce your stress level and muscle tension. A person trains himself or herself to respond to a cue word such as "relax" or "calm" and responds by acting it out. Whenever the individual hears the cue word, he or she will immediately relax. This technique can be used in a variety of situations to help a person to calm down whenever he or she feels like going over the edge.

Rediscovering Values

The fifth technique enables you to rediscover your values. When you remind yourself of your values and purpose, it will help you deal with emotional distress as it comes at you during different moments of your life.

Living in and Affirming the Moment

Another technique is to practice living in the present moment and not thinking about anything else. One way to do that is by using self-affirming statements.

When you are faced with a challenge, you can remind yourself that you have encountered harder situations. You can also say, "I can do this. I have done harder things before. I am strong enough to handle everything that comes my way. Nothing can stop me now."

You can also compliment yourself in a time of difficulty and tell yourself how great you are. You may utter, "You are amazing! You are a great person, and I know that you will get through this because you have so much perseverance and endurance."

Distress tolerance requires the individual to accept the inevitable, as well as the fact that there is nothing else that you can do to change a situation but to live in the present. We should not fight against the current reality; instead, we should accept it for what it is. That does not mean that we approve of what is negative or destructive about it, though. Rather than being able to change the given circumstance, the individual can choose how to respond to it based on his or her true feelings and emotions.

Review the Four Modules of DBP

Now that we have looked at all the four modules for dialectical behavioral therapy, you can see that each one works to help you find the solution when it comes to dealing with your complex emotions.

The first module involves mindfulness. In this book, we have talked about all the different mindfulness and meditation practices that you can do while relaxing so that you have time to think about the present. You can forget everything that is happening outside of your control and focus on your inner world instead. In addition to that, you may concentrate on each moment, as well as the way you think and breathe. When you do this, you will be able to cope with overwhelming feelings that may arise over time. This will allow you to deal with your fears and anxieties and bring a sense of calm in your life.

The second module focuses on learning how to regulate your emotions. As we have discussed earlier, emotions are powerful, and they can cause you to act out in impulsive and sometimes destructive ways. Thus, you really have to monitor your emotions and know when you are starting to get on the edge so that you can respond to them accordingly. Many people with illnesses such as borderline personality disorder have difficulty in controlling their emotions or self-regulation. So, this module teaches you how to monitor your feelings and deal with them when they proceed to get out of whack. Some of the things you should understand include identifying the negative emotion, learning to let go of that feeling, noticing an arousal pattern, and hitting the "pause" button before a situation escalates and gets to the worst point.

The third module emphasizes interpersonal skills, as well as how you can improve with your relationships. This is a crucial aspect for individuals who are living with borderline personality disorder because they might not have the social skills needed to approach, listen to, and handle conflicts constructively with others. The module educates the participants on how to interact with one another peacefully and support each other to achieve a goal-oriented task. It is often is completed in a group therapy setting in which a patient can meet other people with the same disorder and learn how to work in cooperative groups.

The final module involves the practice of distress tolerance. Here, the patient learns how to deal with the reality of emotions and the truth that there are situations that he or she cannot change. Instead, this individual must learn to accept what is happening and roll with it. He or she must not fight the current circumstances; rather, he or she should learn how to coexist with the realities of life. This will help him or her to cope with various emotions that can easily be overwhelming for troubled individuals.

All these modules work together to give a unique cognitive behavioral therapy that helps patients with borderline personality disorder.

Final Thoughts

To summarize what we have discussed in this book, cognitive and dialectical behavior therapies are two forms of psychotherapy that have been proven to help patients cope and thrive with a variety of mental health conditions, including bipolar disorder, anxiety disorders, and borderline personality disorder. They have been useful in the past thirty years and have continued to gain popularity in the world ever since.

There has never been a better time to seek the treatment that you deserve because mental health is slowly losing its stigma. With the media and events such as National Mental Health Month, more people in the United States are becoming more accustomed to talking about the issue of mental health. Many individuals look for treatment to get better. It is only if you check out the available options that you can get well and stay in good condition for the rest of your life. Many people are hesitant to rely on medications that come with serious side effects and cause permanent damage to a person's body. However, there are other options. With CBT and DBT, though, you can get all the treatment that can come from medication and apply it to your life. The bonus is that you can modify your thought patterns so that you will be able to respond to negative thoughts and overpowering feelings constructively and proactively.

Your mental health is a crucial part of your well-being. If you are not well in the mind, then your physical, emotional, and spiritual health will suffer. Therefore, it is vital to find ways to deal with all of life's challenges positively. You need to have a plan. Regardless if you are a patient with bipolar disorder, borderline personality disorder or some other mental health condition, remember that you do not have to suffer alone. Don't endure by yourself without any support. Seek the help of others to get better. We all need someone to help us anyway. We cannot go through this life without the guidance of others who have traveled more than we have.

This book is supposed to be an introduction to the

techniques and tips that are used in CBT and DBT. It has presented information that has been supported by research and psychologists, who are experts in the field. We must say that we have sought to refer to the most reliable sources to be able to provide quality data. This way, you can decide if you would like to pursue treatment from CBT or DBT.

Nevertheless, the book is, by no means, meant to be a substitute for professional treatment with a therapist or other mental health professionals. We want you to use it to learn about techniques that such individuals might use, but we want to encourage you to get the treatment that you need by consulting a trusted counselor who can provide you with the services that will allow you manage your moods and emotions successfully.

Thank you for reading this book. We hope that you have been able to learn many things about CBT and DBT and feel empowered to use the tips and techniques taught to improve your life. Through modifying your thought patterns and behaviors, you will be able to see positive results in your mental health. You should also be able to face your fears, cope with your negative emotions, and live with a can-do attitude. We know that you can achieve your dreams and go through the motions of life if you genuinely want to. With the help of CBT and DBT, though, you may accomplish what once seemed to be impossible: wellness and recovery.

Take care of your mental health; be good and gentle to yourself. After all, you deserve to experience joy and peace in life. Live for the present and leave your cares and anxieties. All will be well.

Bibliography

American Psychiatric Association. (2018). APA public opinion poll – annual meeting 2018. Retrieved from https://www.psychiatry.org/newsroom/apa-public-opinion-poll-annual-meeting-2018

American Psychiatric Association. (n.d.) Diagnostic and Statistical Manual of Mental Disorders (DSM–5). Retrieved from https://www.psychiatry.org/psychiatrists/practice/dsm

Anxiety and Depression Association of America. (n.d.). Understanding the facts of anxiety disorders. Retrieved from https://adaa.org/understanding-anxiety

Beck, A. T. (1976). *Cognitive Therapy and the Emotional Disorders,* New York: Penguin.

Bray, S. (2013). Distress tolerance in dialectical behavior therapy. Retrieved from https://www.goodtherapy.org/blog/distress-tolerance-dialectical-behavior-therapy-0117134

Bray, S. (2013). Interpersonal effectiveness in dialectical behavioral therapy. Retrieved from https://www.goodtherapy.org/blog/interpersonal-effectiveness-dialectical-behavior-therapy-dbt-0416134

Cagliostro, D. (2018). Borderline personality disorder: A guide to spotting the signs of borderline personality disorder - BPD. Retrieved from https://www.psycom.net/depression.central.borderline.html

Caplan, J. E. & Jellinek, M. S. (2009). "Psychotherapy with

Children and Adolescents." Developmental-Behavioral Pediatrics (Fourth Edition). Elsevier.

Clark, D. A. (2005). Intrusive thoughts in clinical disorders: Theory, research, and treatment. Guilford Publications.

Cullen, M., Brito Pons, G. & Mindful Staff. (2016). Mindfulness of anger. Retrieved from https://www.mindful.org/mindfulness-of-anger/

Fenn, K. & Byrne, M. (2013). The key principles of cognitive behavioural therapy. InnovAiT, 6(9), 579–585. https://doi.org/10.1177/1755738012471029

Grohol, J. M. (2018). An overview of dialectical behavior therapy. Retrieved from https://psychcentral.com/lib/an-overview-of-dialectical-behavior-therapy/

Klinger, E. (1978–1979). Dimensions of thought and imagery in normal waking states. *Journal of Altered States of Consciousness*, 4, 97–113.

Klinger, E. & Cox, W. M. (1987–1988). Dimensions of thought flow in everyday life. *Imagination, Cognition and Personality*, 7, 105–128.

Klinger, E. (1996). "Emotional influences on cognitive processing, with implications for theories of both," in *The Psychology of Action: Linking Cognition and Motivation to Behavior* eds Gollwitzer P., Bargh J. A., editors. New York: Guilford Press, p. 168–189.

Linehan, M. (1993). Cognitive-behavioral treatment of borderline personality disorder. New York: Guilford Press, p. 3.

Linehan, M. (2001). Dialectical behavioral therapy. Retreived from https://www.sciencedirect.com/topics/nursing-and-health-professions/dialectical-behavior-therapy

National Institute of Mental Health. (2018). Depression. Retrieved from https://www.nimh.nih.gov/health/topics/depression/index.shtml

Padesky, C. (1993). Socratic questioning: changing minds or guiding discovery? Keynote address delivered at European Association for Behavioural and Cognitive Psychotherapies Conference, *London*, UK.

Positive Psychology Program: Your One-Stop Positive Psychology Resource. (2017). 22 mindfulness exercises, techniques, and activities for adults (+PDFs). Retrieved from https://positivepsychologyprogram.com/mindfulness-exercises-techniques-activities

Positive Psychology Program: Your One-Stop Positive Psychology Resource. (2018). Emotion regulation worksheets & strategies: Improve your DBT skills. Retrieved from https://positivepsychologyprogram.com/emotion-regulation-worksheets-strategies-dbt-skills/

Positive Psychology Program: Your One-Stop Positive Psychology Resource. (2019). Interpersonal effectiveness: 9 worksheets & examples. Retrieved from https://positivepsychologyprogram.com/interpersonal-effectiveness/

Powers Lott, A. & Stenson, A. (n.d.). Types of anxiety.

Retrieved from https://www.anxiety.org/what-is-anxiety

Psychology Today. (n.d.). Dialectical behavior therapy. Retrieved from https://www.psychologytoday.com/us/therapy-types/dialectical-behavior-therapy

Rachman, S. (1981). Part 1. Unwanted intrusive cognitions. *Advances in Behaviour Research and Therapy*, 3, 89–99.

Reddy, M. S. & Vijay, M. S. (2017). Empirical reality of dialectical behavioral therapy in borderline personality. *Indian Journal of Psychological Medicine*, 39(2), 105-108.

Salkovskis, P. M. (1988). Intrusive thoughts and obsessional disorders. In D. Glasgow & N. Eisenberg (Eds.), Current issues in clinical psychology (Vol. 4). London: Gower.

Salters-Pedneault, K. (2018). Understanding borderline personality disorder (BPD). Retrieved from https://www.verywellmind.com/what-is-borderline-personality-disorder-bpd-425487

Schimelpfening, N. (2019). Overview of dialectical behavioral therapy. Retrieved from https://www.verywellmind.com/dialectical-behavior-therapy-1067402

Singer, J. (1998). Daydreams, the stream of consciousness, and self-representations. In R. Bornstein & L. Masling (Eds.), Empirical perspectives on the psychoanalytic unconscious. Empirical studies of psychoanalytic theories (Vol. 7, pp. 141–186). Washington, DC: American Psychological Association.

Skyland Trail. (2017). 4 differences between CBT and DBT and how to tell which is right for you. Retrieved from https://www.skylandtrail.org/About/Blog/ctl/ArticleView/mid/567/articleId/6747/4-Differences-Between-CBT-and-DBT-and-How-to-Tell-Which-is-Right-for-You

Spradlin, S.E. (2003). *Don't let your emotions run your life: How dialectical behavior therapy can put you in control.* Oakland, CA: New Harbinger Publications, Inc.

Sunrise Residential Treatment Center. (2017). What are DBT emotion regulation skills? Retrieved from https://www.sunrisertc.com/dbt-emotion-regulation-skills/

van Rooij, S. & Stenson, A. (n.d.). An introduction to anxiety. Retrieved from https://www.anxiety.org/what-is-anxiety

World Health Organization. (2017). Depression and other common mental disorders - Global health estimates. Retrieved from https://apps.who.int/iris/bitstream/handle/10665/254610/WHO-MSD-MER-2017.2-eng.pdf?sequence=1

www.ingramcontent.com/pod-product-compliance
Ingram Content Group UK Ltd.
Pitfield, Milton Keynes, MK11 3LW, UK
UKHW022224230426

12048UKWH00016BA/1055